FALSELY ACCUSED

by
Neil Snyder

Neil Snyder

Contents

About the Author

Neil Snyder taught at the University of Virginia for 25 years before retiring in 2004 and moving to Lake Hartwell in South Carolina. He is the author of numerous books including Vision, Values & Courage (The Free Press, 1994) and The Will to Lead (Irwin Professional Publishing, 1997). He has published more than 100 articles and business case studies. Currently, he is the Ralph A. Beeton Professor of Free Enterprise Emeritus at the University of Virginia.

During his tenure at UVA, Dr. Snyder served as Policy Advisor for Regulatory Reform to Governor Charles S. Robb of Virginia (1982-1985); he was co-chairman in 1985 and chairman in 1986 of the Governor's Conference on Small Business in Virginia; and in 1985, he received the Small Business Advocacy Award of the Virginia Chamber of Commerce. He has worked with GE, the Federal Bureau of Investigation, the Drug Enforcement Administration, and the Department of Defense, among others.

Chapter 1
A Shooting in South Carolina

September 8, 2006 wasn't a typical day for me and my wife, Katie. We were busy taking care of last minute details before leaving the country for a two month stay in Israel. I was too preoccupied with completing my do list to pay close attention to the news in Upstate South Carolina where we live, but an unusual shooting incident that day attracted so much local media coverage that I couldn't help hearing about it.

The so-called "murder victim" was a pregnant woman whose baby was delivered postmortem. The infant was in critical condition from the moment she was born. She was rushed to a neonatal unit in Spartanburg, South Carolina where she was kept alive on machines for 40 days before dying. She never took an unassisted breath.

****

In late October 2007, more than a year after the shooting, I spent several days playing golf with a good friend from my high school and college days. I don't think I even turned on the television while he was in town. I know that I didn't read the local newspaper. Truth is I never actually read the local paper. I scan it, quickly. Katie's our designated local paper reader. I get my news from the Internet.

On October 25, 2007, it's no wonder that I didn't read, hear, or see anything in the local media having to do with the acquittal of a young woman who had been accused of committing a double homicide, but things were about to change. Following a remarkable series of events in early January 2008, my attention was drawn to the facts of the case because it looked as though the shooter had been victimized by an overzealous prosecutor. I decided to investigate and find out if there was a story that needed to be told.

****

Since I knew almost nothing about the case, I called the local newspaper office in Anderson, South Carolina—the town where the shooting took place—and asked the receptionist at the *Anderson Independent-Mail* for help. She forwarded my call to Pearce Adams. He covered the trial for the paper.

Pearce gave me the information I needed to get started. For instance, he told me that Cynthia Marchbanks was the acquitted woman's name. He didn't know where she lived or even if she still lived in town, but simply telling me her name was helpful. When I told Pearce that I was thinking about writing a book about the shooting, he said, "That should be a great book."

"I think you're right," I said, but I was just making small talk because I didn't know enough about the case at that time to carry on an intelligent conversation. I was about to learn, though.

The next step was simple but tedious. I started calling every Marchbanks in the Anderson phone book. One-by-one I asked, "Do you know Cynthia Marchbanks?" until finally a voice on the other end of the line said, "She's my granddaughter."

When I told Mrs. Marchbanks that I wanted to write a book about her granddaughter's case, she started crying. I thought, *Oh no. I've really messed up now.* That wasn't the case at all. She was still suffering emotionally from the nightmare that her family had been forced to endure; only their ordeal wasn't a dream. She wanted to talk about it. She needed to talk about it, and I was ready to listen. The things she told me are included in this book, and there's more, much more.

Mrs. Marchbanks said something that day that made a lasting impression on me. She said, "I've been guilty of reading newspaper articles about people accused of committing crimes or seeing reports on TV about them and believing that they were guilty based on nothing more than news coverage. This experience has taught me never to do that. My granddaughter was made out to be a murderer by the local media, but she's not."

Then she told me that she would ask Cyndi, not Cynthia, to give me a call. A few days later, Mrs. Marchbanks called and asked me to contact Cyndi's lawyer, Druanne White. I think it's fair to say that Cyndi was a little skeptical. After what she had been put through, I don't blame her. She wanted Druanne to check me out before meeting with me.

Like good lawyers always do, Druanne asked me lots of questions. For instance,

- "Have you ever written a book?" Yes, several.
- "How much do you know about Cyndi's case?" Practically nothing.
- "Have you ever written a book like this one?" No, but I'm looking forward to writing it.

Druanne had other questions, and I must have answered them well enough because her last question was "When do you want to meet?"

****

To write this book properly, I needed lots of detailed information from Cyndi, information that only she could provide. But what if I found out that the jury made a mistake and that she was actually guilty of murder? What conditions or restrictions would Druanne and Cyndi want to impose on me? I knew that I couldn't accept any constraints at all.

Or what if Cyndi wanted a percentage of the royalties from the book? That wouldn't work either because if she and I were partners on the book, in the eyes of critics my objectivity would be suspect, at best. Given the media attention that her case generated, I knew that I had to scrupulously avoid even the perception of impropriety.

I met with Druanne and Cyndi that Saturday for lunch, and they agreed to give me all the information they had including direct access to Cyndi for as long as it took to answer all of my questions. Before the book was finished, I interviewed Cyndi numerous times. If I had questions between meetings, I called her and she answered them. Druanne made time available for me in her busy schedule as well. And what did they require from me in return? Nothing at all and that's the way it had to be.

It shocked our community when news of the shooting started circulating, but the exculpatory details of the incident never got out. This book tells what actually happened, and I didn't want to destroy my credibility by giving detractors easy targets at which to aim. Any concession on my part, no matter how trivial, could have been made into an issue by naysayers.

****

This is a story about a young woman who was accused of crimes that she didn't commit—serious crimes that could have landed her in prison for the rest of her life. The jury saw the evidence and the truth, and they reached a not guilty verdict, but they couldn't undo the damage done to Cyndi and her family by members of the law enforcement community in Anderson, South Carolina who had to ignore powerful exonerative evidence to even bring charges against her. Before Cyndi's case went to trial, they had to close their eyes to evidence from South Carolina's forensic lab that vindicated her.

Any parent will find this story interesting, but it's the kind of thing that young people need to read as well. They don't want to repeat Cyndi's mistakes.

That's right. Cyndi did not commit a crime because she acted in self-defense, but she did shoot and kill her pregnant friend. The baby died too. Cyndi will have to live with that for the rest of her life. She made several other mistakes—the kind that young people are prone to make. For example, she was naïve; she was foolish about a number of things; and she was too trusting. More than anything else, she let her desire to help a desperate friend interfere with her judgment, and it led to terrible and avoidable consequences.

Today, Cyndi knows that she made mistakes, but she's not the same person she was on September 8, 2006. Facing a charge of double homicide and looking at the possibility of spending the rest of your life in the state penitentiary has a way of forcing you to grow up in a hurry.

Katie and I have two daughters. I remember them doing things when they were younger that made no sense to me. Sometimes I would get angry, raise my voice, and say things that I now regret. But I made similar mistakes when I was young. My parents had to suffer through my transition from adolescence to adulthood. I'll bet you made mistakes as well. Keep that in mind as you read this book, and don't judge Cyndi too harshly.

****

Before you read any further, I need to give you a warning. There is some foul language in this book that many of you will find offensive. It's not gratuitous. They're the words that were actually used, and I didn't try to sanitize the story for sensitive ears.

It's a sad commentary on our times, but the gutter language I've let in, as revolting as it is, isn't unfamiliar to you or to your children. You hear it at school, on the streets, on television, and in movie theaters. If you own a satellite radio, you hear it there as well. It also contains gruesome details of a bloody shooting. That, too, couldn't be avoided.

This is a book that you and your children need to read. Don't let the language and the gory details stop you from recommending it to them.

Chapter 2

No Good Deed Goes Unpunished

There are momentous days in our lives when the world we know changes completely. Nothing can ever be the same again. Like B.C. and A.D., they divide our time on earth into two distinct parts—before this and after this. More often than not, we don't appreciate their significance until they're distant memories. At her young age, Cyndi Marchbanks can already point to two of those days—one an ill-fated day when her world came crashing down and the other a day when she was given another chance.

****

It started out innocently enough. It was a simple request from a childhood friend, but there was a sense of urgency and a touch of desperation in Amber Robey's voice that Cyndi Marchbanks couldn't ignore. The boyfriend of Cyndi's middle school pal was abusing drugs, and her. Amber said that she needed a place to stay, someplace far away where she could start a new life without Mike Jackson, the father of her two-year-old son, Hunter, and her unborn daughter. She told Cyndi that Mike had taken advantage of her long enough.

Cyndi didn't hesitate. She knew she had to lend Amber a helping hand.

In less than a month, Amber would be dead from a gunshot wound to the face. Her unborn daughter, Hailey, would be taken from her lifeless body via Caesarean section and kept alive on machines for 40 days until doctors pulled the plug and declared her dead. Cyndi Marchbanks, an intelligent and attractive 22-year-old woman who just three weeks earlier had been satisfied with her life, would be locked up in Anderson County Detention Center (ACDC) facing a

10

charge of double homicide. The punishment could be the death penalty or life in prison without the chance of parole.

Unceremoniously, Cyndi was fired by her manager at the Anderson, South Carolina O'Charley's, a chain restaurant with home offices in Nashville, Tennessee. He told her that he was ordered to do it by headquarters executives because she had failed to call in or to report to work, from jail. Ironically, Cyndi had just been promoted and given management responsibilities.

And for the pièce de résistance, Cyndi became the focal point of a media feeding frenzy accompanying the high-profile "murder case." In the eyes of many people in the Anderson community, it transformed the demure and relatively unknown young woman into a notorious celebrity, a hideous monster, the cold-blooded killer of a mother and her unborn child.

These examples of sensational headlines following the shooting focused people's attention on the alleged murderer:

- "Marchbanks Gave Victim Ride Minutes Before Shooting"
- "Family Calls Bond for Marchbanks 'Slap in Face'"
- "Marchbanks Charged with Murder in Baby Hailey's Death"

****

In 1997, twelve-year-old Cyndi Marchbanks moved with her parents from Anderson, South Carolina to Chesapeake Beach, Maryland. The children in her 7th grade class at Plum Point Middle School had been together for more than five months by the time Cyndi arrived, and cliques had formed already.

Cyndi was the new kid in town, the one from the Deep South with the thick Southern drawl. She wasn't the kind of youngster everyone wanted to make friends with right away. Amber Robey wasn't part of the in crowd. She was tall for her age, overweight, and aggressive. She didn't fit in either. Cyndi was okay by her, and quickly they became middle school buddies.

Cyndi's friendship with Amber at that young age had a lot to do with the mistakes she made in the summer of 2006. In Cyndi's mind, she was indebted to Amber for taking her in when others in her class wouldn't. As far as Cyndi was concerned, she was just returning a favor or repaying a debt. In retrospect, she knows that she made a tragic error, but as they say, hindsight is 20/20.

"Even though we were close friends in middle school," Cyndi recalled, "I spent the night at Amber's house only once. When my mother met her father, she almost had a heart attack. He was a biker—motorcycles. He had tattoos, a ponytail, and a handlebar mustache, and he wore a bandana around his head."

Amber told Cyndi that her mother and father used illegal drugs on a regular basis. Cyndi's mother guessed as much, and she never allowed Cyndi to spend the night with Amber again.

At age 13, Amber was too young to buy cigarettes on her own so her parents bought them for her. "Amber smoked at her house," Cyndi said, "but my mother wouldn't let Amber smoke at our house, so she never spent the night with me."

"Amber was a bully. She lost all control when she was angry. The other kids were afraid of her. No one messed with Amber, not even her father. He used to clean houses. One day he asked Amber to help him, and he said that he would pay her. When they finished cleaning the houses, Amber demanded her money on the spot. Her father told her that he would pay her when he got paid. Amber threatened to 'trash' all the houses they had cleaned if he didn't pay her right then. That little father-daughter quarrel almost turned into a free-for-all."

"Amber threatened me only once. My parents gave me a guitar for Christmas, and Amber said she would break in the strings and tune it for me. About three months later, I learned that my guitar was broken. Amber wouldn't fix it or pay for it. She wouldn't even tell me how it happened. When I asked her about it, she said, 'I'm going to whip your ass.' I decided not to press the issue. If Amber said she was going to beat you up, she meant it. I was well aware of Amber's reputation as a ruthless fighter. I saw her fight several times. She deserved that reputation. To avoid a confrontation, I apologized to her, and she never threatened me again—that is she never threatened me again until September 8, 2006."

****

Despite their occasional differences, the two girls remained close friends throughout middle school. If you're a parent, you may be wondering what Cyndi's mother and father could have done to prevent Cyndi from seeing Amber. If you have, or have had, teenage children, you already know the answer—not much. Ordering Cyndi not to see Amber would have been a mistake. She would almost certainly have rebelled and seen more of Amber because Amber was her only friend.

By the time she started high school, Cyndi had other friends. She and Amber saw each other in the halls and talked now and then, but they didn't spend much time together. They weren't close pals like they had been in middle school.

Following high school graduation, Cyndi moved to Orlando, Florida and eventually back to Anderson, South Carolina so she could be near her boyfriend, Justin Bond. Amber stayed in Maryland and became involved with Mike Jackson. She had one child by him, and another one was on the way during the summer of 2006.

As the years went by, Amber telephoned Cyndi about once a month. "Each time we talked, it seemed like Amber was facing another crisis. It was obvious to me that her life was beginning to spin out of control. She was getting frantic, desperate. I could hear it in her voice."

****

"In the summer of 2006, things changed dramatically. Amber started calling me at least 2 or 3 times a week. She said things were getting worse by the day. She talked about how unlucky she was and how unhappy she was with Mike. She told me that Mike refused to get a job or do anything to help her. According to Amber, all he wanted to do was get high and deal drugs."

"Mike and Amber lived with Amber's parents in Maryland for a while, and they shared the rent. Amber said that Mike sold PCP, crack, and cocaine out of their home. When Amber's mother found out what Mike was doing, she was furious. Amber said she was angry because Mike didn't sell anything to her. Obviously, they weren't your typical American family."

Amber told Cyndi that eventually her parents went to live with her grandparents in Waynesboro, Virginia. When they moved out, Amber had to pay all of the rent because the house was leased in her name. "Amber said her parents had bad credit. That prevented them from renting a house in their own names. Amber had to work long hours to come up with the $2500 a month she needed to pay their bills. She kept telling me that Mike wouldn't lift a finger to help her."

"Amber and Mike tried to save money by living with other relatives, but that didn't work out. The welcome mats were taken in by his family and hers. Amber's grandparents in Virginia kicked her out when a drug pipe fell out of her purse. Her grandparents took a firm stand against drug use. When they saw that drug pipe, Amber had to go."

As the summer of 2006 was drawing to a close, Amber told Cyndi that she was thinking about having an abortion. She was 6 months pregnant and someone showed her an ultrasound image of the baby. That did it. She decided to have the child. "I thought if Amber moved to South Carolina I could help her get off drugs and have a healthy baby," Cyndi said. "That's the main reason I wanted her to come down here."

Amber and Cyndi talked about many things as the summer wore on. Nothing they discussed turned out to be more illuminating than the stories Amber told about violent brawls in parking lots outside honkytonks and bars. "She fought grown men," Cyndi said as tears welled up in her eyes, "often several at a time, and she won. According to Amber, she and Mike fought all the time—bar fights mostly, but sometimes they fought each other."

Cyndi shook her head slowly and paused for a moment as she stared at nothing in particular. "She meant fist fights. I've seen Amber and Mike go at it. They hit each other in the face, hard. One time I saw Mike hit Amber in the face right in front of her father, and her father didn't say a word—nothing at all. She was about 5 feet 8 inches tall, and she weighed at least 225 pounds. Mike is more than 6 feet tall, and he must weigh 250 pounds or more, but he's not fat like she was. He's just big, really big. I couldn't believe it." Cyndi was wiping tears away from her eyes as she thought about that fight.

"Amber had other problems, too. She told me that she was shooting up cocaine. There's no telling how much damage she did to her unborn baby. I told Amber she should stop doing drugs, but she wouldn't listen. I guess I should have known that I couldn't help her, but I didn't. At least I didn't know it at that time. It became obvious to me later on, though."

"Amber told me that she wanted to get away from Mike, but she didn't have anywhere to go. She asked me about moving to South Carolina. It costs a lot less to rent a house down here. I told her that she could live with Justin and me in our house rent free on two conditions. She had to leave Mike and there could be no drugs. I even told her to bring Hunter if she wanted to. In the end, Mike came with her. That was a huge mistake."

Amber's decision to bring Mike with her to South Carolina still haunts Cyndi. "She wasn't stable to start with, and having him here sponging off of her made things worse. Amber had enough problems without him. He neglected her and abused her physically, and he was a parasite. He was so lazy that he wouldn't even help her bring groceries in from the car, but Amber brought him with her anyway. That didn't make any sense to me."

Cyndi arranged for Amber to rent the house next door to her for $400 a month. If Mike wasn't around, she thought she could make a difference in Amber's life, but she was wrong. To begin with, Amber didn't come without Mike. That was a terrible mistake, and in the end, she didn't want Cyndi's help.

****

Looking back on it, August 19, 2006 is a day Cyndi Marchbanks wishes had never happened because that's the day Amber Robey, Mike Jackson, their son Hunter, and Amber's father arrived in Anderson, South Carolina. "As soon as I saw Amber, I knew she was high on something. Her pupils were dilated and she looked and acted like she was stoned. I asked her what she had taken, but she denied using any drugs. Later that evening, she admitted that she and Mike stayed up all night the night before and finished off their entire stash of cocaine."

"Mike Jackson's arrival was a complete surprise. I had no idea he was coming. When I saw him get out of the car, it broke my heart. Mike wasn't Amber's only problem, but I think he was a big part of every problem she had. He did nothing to help her."

"On their first day in town, Amber asked me to help her get some 'weed.' That's marijuana," she told me as if I didn't already know. "Amber told me she was experiencing cocaine withdrawal and that the marijuana would help her get through it. She even said the withdrawal could kill her baby. That was ridiculous, but that's what she said. I told her the drugs would hurt her baby, but she ignored me. Right away, Mike started asking me to connect him up with someone who could sell him several pounds of marijuana. He wanted to deal drugs out of the house next door to mine. I told him 'NO!' I knew then that I was going to have some problems to deal with, but I thought I could handle them. Obviously, I couldn't."

16

****

The next day, Amber's father drove back to Virginia, and he took Hunter with him. Since Amber and Mike didn't have a car, Cyndi became their chauffeur. That turned out to be a heavy load.

Before moving to South Carolina, Amber paid the power deposit, so they had electricity when they arrived. On their first full day in town, Cyndi drove Amber to the gas company and the water company to pay deposits. "Amber paid the gas deposit," Cyndi said, "but when we got to the water company, she cussed the people out because she didn't have enough money for a deposit. She told them it was too high. Then she ordered me to take her back to the gas company so she could get a refund on that deposit. They closed her account but told her that they would have to mail her a check. She was furious."

Amber and Mike lived next door to Cyndi and Justin for three weeks with no running water and no gas. They did have cable television, though, and according to Cyndi, they didn't pay for it. "They just hooked up their 32 inch flat screen TV to the existing line. They took showers at our house, and Amber hauled water from our house in 5-gallon buckets so they could flush their toilet and have drinking water. During the day, they watched TV, and Mike played on his X-box."

Because they didn't have water or a washer and dryer, Cyndi became Amber's and Mike's personal valet. "At first, Amber brought their laundry over to my house. I washed, dried, and folded their clothes and returned them to Amber's house. Mike made Amber carry the laundry over. It was heavy so I started going to get it."

Amber needed a job so Cyndi introduced her to Angela, her boss at O'Charley's. "Angela hired Amber because I vouched for her, and she let Amber hostess because she was pregnant. The hostess doesn't have to move around very much. That was the perfect job for Amber. Our daily routine was simple. I worked the day shift, and Amber worked the evening shift. As quickly as I got home from work, I drove Amber to work. Then I picked her up from work when her shift ended. It wasn't easy, and it took a lot of time and gas, but we were getting by."

"I tried to get Mike a job too, so he wouldn't have an excuse to sell drugs. It was a construction job, and the foreman said Mike could have a job if he came to work the next morning ready to go. I drove Mike to the site at 7:00. He was wearing flip-flops with socks. That didn't go over very well with the foreman. You should have seen his expression when he saw Mike. He just looked at him and told him to hit the road. It was obvious to me that Mike didn't want a job."

"In the evenings, Amber and Mike liked to hang around our house, and they stayed until we went to bed. They would sit in our living room and brag about all the bar fights they'd been in and the drugs they took. Day after day after day, that's all I heard about—bar fights and drugs, bar fights and drugs. It was scary, and it got old in a hurry. I didn't have any reason to doubt what they were saying, and Amber was 6 months pregnant. I know it's hard to believe, but that's what they said. What kind of person would fight a pregnant woman?"

****

Cyndi is the kind of friend all of us wish we had. She was willing to turn her own life upside-down and ignore her personal needs to help out her old friend Amber. Justin didn't like the way Amber and Mike treated Cyndi, and for good reason. He told her about it, daily. Even so, Cyndi felt a strong sense of obligation that she refused to ignore.

When I think about what Cyndi did for Amber and Mike, I remember all the times I've complained about having to go a little bit out of my way to get something for someone because I was in a hurry. I'm picking on myself, but I know every one of us has been guilty of doing the same thing at one time or another.

While Cyndi was telling me how much she did for Amber and Mike, I found it difficult to believe—a little over the top as far as I was concerned. I don't want to get ahead of myself, but as you will see later, that's exactly what Mike Jackson said from the witness stand, and he was the prosecution's star witness. Cyndi's neighbors said the same thing. I was learning an important lesson, a lesson I needed to understand in order to write this book. Cyndi didn't exaggerate or fabricate. She always told me the unvarnished truth, even when it cast her in a bad light.

"Looking back on it," Cyndi said, "I realize that I gave Amber too much leeway—way too much, but at the time it seemed like the right thing to do. Having spent so many years apart, I didn't fully appreciate the changes that had taken place in Amber's life. She wasn't the same person I knew in middle school, and things got worse by the day after she moved to Anderson."

****

In February 2008, Cyndi was sitting in our living room doing her best to make sense of what happened. By that time, her trial had been over for about 3 months and she had had time to reflect on the whole ordeal. "Amber was resentful. She was very unhappy and things were getting worse. I believe that's why she was so angry and negative all the time. Amber shot down anything I said. She snapped at me over anything no matter how trivial it was. It finally got to the point where she would fly off the handle at me over nothing at all. She would go from zero-to-pissed in a second. I could tell she had reached the boiling point and was about ready to explode."

"Here's an example of what I'm talking about. Angela, my manager at O'Charley's, had already told Amber not to wear shirts to work that showed her armpits. If you work at a restaurant, you can't wear shirts like that. That wasn't news to Amber. She had worked in restaurants before."

"A few days before the incident, Amber came over to my house for me to take her to work, and she was wearing one of those shirts. I looked at her and said, 'Amber, you can't wear that shirt. Angela told you that already.'"

"Amber stomped out of the house in a huff and slammed the door behind her, hard. I mean she rattled the hinges. She was gone for about 10 minutes. I didn't know what to do. Should I call Angela and tell her that Amber wasn't coming in, or what? I didn't know. I was getting ready to make the call when Amber came back over still in a rage. She stormed into my living room and yelled at me, 'You can't talk to me that way.'"

"What are you talking about? You don't want to get fired over a shirt, do you?"

"I don't care," she said angrily. "You still can't talk to me that way. Who do you think you are?"

"I didn't know how to respond, so I just said, 'I'm not trying to be ugly.'"

"That's petty. That's stupid," Amber said. "If they're going to fire me over a shirt, maybe I don't need to work there."

"Why would Amber try to make a big deal out of something that unimportant? She knew the rules as well as I did. Each day, she was getting more moody and more unpredictable. I think she was just trying to pick a fight with me. I was beginning to get nervous around her. I was doing everything I could to help her, but the more I did, the angrier she got. What could I do at that point? I hoped things would get better, but they never did. In fact, they kept getting worse."

****

"I knew Amber was taking advantage of me. Justin knew it better than I did, and he reminded me about it every night when we went to bed. Still, I had mixed feelings when Amber told me that she and Mike were moving. Part of me wanted to jump in the air, scream for joy, and shout halleluyah, but I also wanted her to stay here, solve her problems, and deliver a healthy baby. I could tell she wasn't making any progress. Amber thought everybody was trying to do something to her, like the whole world was against her and she had no hope."

"I tried to tell Amber that she could accomplish anything if she was willing to work. It didn't make any difference what I said. She just brushed it off, and she always had a sullen look on her face. Amber refused to accept responsibility for anything, and increasingly she directed her anger toward me, as if I was to blame for her predicament. Well, she ended up dumping her problems on me, and now they really are my problems. I'll have to live with them for the rest of my life."

"Finally, Amber told me that she and Mike were catching the bus the next day. She said that she had had enough. Before leaving town, they wanted to sell their television set to a nearby pawnbroker. Amber thought it would fetch a good price, but she didn't have any idea how pawnshops work. The pawnshop is less than two miles from my house so I agreed to drive them over there the next morning before work. September 8, 2006, that's the day Amber and Mike were supposed to catch the bus. It's the worst day of my life."

Chapter 3

The Worst Day of My Life

To make sense of what happened on September 8, 2006, you need to look at it in context. It was the culmination of three very difficult weeks for Amber Robey, and it followed closely on the heels of several months of drug and physical abuse. The helpmate who came to Anderson, South Carolina with Amber, Mike Jackson, turned out to be anything but.

"Bringing Mike with her was the worst mistake Amber could have made," Cyndi said. "He was an emotional and a financial drag on her. I believe he pushed her over the edge."

"On top of everything else, Amber was having trouble at work. She wasn't getting many shifts at O'Charley's, so she wasn't earning enough money to make ends meet. She was new, but that wasn't her problem. She had a bad attitude, and no one wanted to work with her. She wasn't happy. She didn't smile at the customers or greet them the way a hostess should. Amber wasn't a good hostess so the managers limited her hours as much as they could. Her father sent them some money to help them make ends meet, but not enough. Amber and Mike were in trouble financially, and she knew it."

"A couple of days before the incident, the manager at O'Charley's sent Amber home because he didn't need her that day. That's not unusual in the restaurant business, but it was the last straw as far as Amber was concerned. She decided to quit, but she didn't tell anyone at work. She just called her father and told him that things weren't panning out. He said she could move to Virginia and live with her grandparents again as long as Mike didn't come with her. He even sent them money so they could buy bus tickets. Amber was going to Virginia, and Mike was heading back to Maryland."

"I think Amber's world had finally come unglued. She was emotionally disturbed, physically abused, financially destitute, and pregnant. That's a terrible combination. Still, she refused to accept any personal responsibility for her situation."

Cyndi found herself squarely in the middle of Amber's mess, and she got there on her own volition. She was trying to help a friend. By the time she realized how desperate the situation was, it was too late. The best she could hope for at that point was for Amber and Mike to get on the bus and leave town. They would have, too, that day, but things didn't work out as planned.

"I cry every time I think about it," Cyndi said. "I had known Amber since I was 12 years old, been friends with her all those years. I can't imagine wanting to hurt her. That never entered my mind. It wasn't even in the realm of possibility."

****

Friday September 8, 2006 started out like any other summer day in Anderson—hot and humid. Cyndi had to be at work early, so she needed to take Amber and Mike to the pawnshop first thing in the morning. After three weeks of chauffeuring them all over town, that wasn't a problem. In fact, it was a relief for Cyndi because it would all be over in a matter of hours, or so she thought.

Cyndi was still in her pajamas when she drove her car to Amber's and Mike's house shortly before 9:00 a.m. To make loading the television set as easy as possible, Cyndi positioned the car in their yard so the passenger side front door was near their front porch steps.

As Cyndi walked toward the porch, she could hear Amber and Mike screaming at each other. That wasn't unusual. It made Cyndi feel uncomfortable, but she didn't dwell on it because she was in a hurry. She needed to get back home in time to take a shower and get dressed for work.

Mike opened the door as quickly as Cyndi knocked. He brought the television set out and loaded it in the front passenger seat. Mike and Cyndi waited in the car for Amber, but for some reason she was taking a long time. While they waited, Amber kept screaming at Mike from inside the house. Finally, she came outside and joined Mike in the backseat. According to Cyndi, Amber and Mike quarreled all the way to the pawnshop.

"I drove them over there in my pajamas. When we got to the pawnshop, Mike took the television set inside and left the door open. Amber went inside with him. I was embarrassed, but I got out of the car in my pajamas to close the door. That's when I noticed a tear in my window tinting. Obviously, Mike had scraped it with the television set when he put it in the front seat or when he took it out. I was irritated, but I wasn't mad."

"When Amber walked out of the pawnshop, I could tell something was wrong. She didn't say anything. It was the way she walked—almost stomping, and the way she dropped her eyebrows and stared straight ahead as if she wanted to bite someone's head off."

****

You'll recall that Cyndi said she thought Amber resented her. That may have been the case, but there are other plausible explanations for Amber's erratic behavior. For instance, it's possible that she was jealous of Cyndi. From Amber's point of view, it probably looked as though Cyndi had everything she wanted. Jealousy would have been a normal human response, especially for someone who was in the throes of pregnancy, insolvency, and an unhappy relationship with the father of her infant son and her unborn daughter.

It's also possible that Amber's violent mood swings were caused by a mental problem of some sort—possibly schizophrenia or maybe drug-induced schizophrenia. That's not out of the question given her heavy drug use.

According to research done at the M.I.N.D. (Medical Investigation of Neurodevelopmental Disorders) Institute at the University of California at Davis, drug-induced psychoses probably account for a large number of schizophrenia cases. There's a lot of research supporting that hypothesis. My purpose in bringing this up is simply to point out that Amber's problems may have been much more serious than Cyndi or anyone else imagined.

Whatever the cause may have been, Amber Robey's volatile disposition was clearly on display September 8, 2006. I went to EZ Pawn and talked with the woman who waited on Amber and Mike that morning. She told me that they were in a jovial mood. They even joked with her about needing to sell their television set so they would have enough money to leave town. Cyndi's description suggests that Amber's mood changed completely as soon as she walked out of the pawnshop and looked at her. I've known people personally who were that unpredictable. I'm sure you have too. I'm not a psychiatrist, but I think that kind of behavior is indicative of a deep-seated, underlying problem.

****

"Amber got into the front seat next to me," Cyndi said. "Mike sat in the backseat. Amber didn't say a word as we drove off, and her expression never changed. She just stared out the window. I thought she was looking at the ripped tinting, so I said, 'That's where your TV tore my tint.'"

"Slowly, Amber turned her head and fixed her gaze on me. The look on her face was terrifying. It was pure rage. I could see the hate in her eyes. I could almost feel her intimidating stare. If looks could kill, I would have been dead on the spot. I broke out in a cold sweat, and it was hot that morning."

Neil Snyder

"Later, I learned that the pawnbroker had given them $40 for the television set. Amber had expected more than that, much more, at least a couple of hundred dollars. That may have had something to do with her attitude; I don't know. Whatever the cause was, I was about to become the target of her wrath."

"With a cold, ominous rhythm in her voice, Amber said, 'Here we go. Here we fucking go. You talk a lot of shit. Do you want to start something with me you stupid bitch? Your tint won't take five dollars to fix. I'll give you the fucking five dollars, and you can get it fixed at Wal-Mart.'"

"With each word, Amber's voice grew louder until she was yelling at me. I knew that I had better control my voice. Amber was about to explode. I could feel it. I could see it in her eyes. I didn't want to make her any angrier than she was already. I started thinking, *If I can just get home, drop them off, and go to work, everything will be fine. By the time I get home from work, they'll be gone.*"

"I said, 'Amber, I don't want your money. I've never taken any money from you. I've given you money. The most I would ever want from you is an apology.'"

"Fuck that. Fuck that," Amber said angrily. She squinted her eyes and stared straight at Cyndi.

I could tell that Cyndi was nervous as she explained what happened. Just thinking about the incident scared her more than a year after the episode took place.

"By then, we were at the intersection of highways 81 and 28 less than a mile from my house. I was in the far right lane. While we were stopped at the red light, Amber started yanking on the door handle...hard, so hard that I thought she was going to tear it off. My car doors lock automatically when the transmission is in drive, so the door wouldn't open. She just kept yanking on the door handle anyway."

26

"All of a sudden, Amber started yelling at me hysterically. 'Let me out. Let me out of this fucking car. Let me out of this fucking car right now. Sometimes you can be such a bitch.' She kept getting louder and louder."

"I unlocked the doors and said, 'Okay, get out.' During the trial, the prosecutor would say that I threw Amber out of my car, but that's not true. I let her out because she was about to destroy my door handle. She demanded that I let her out."

"Amber pushed the door open, climbed out of the car, and stomped away. She didn't even close the door. After she walked a few feet, she turned around, walked back to the car, leaned inside, stared at me, and said, 'I'm going to beat your fucking little ass down before you go to work today. You can count on it.'"

"I was scared to death. Mike was still in the backseat. He was laughing hard like it was the funniest thing he had ever seen. I looked back at him and said, 'What's so funny? Your girlfriend is pregnant. Are you going to walk with her or not?'"

"I did throw Mike out of the car. I told him, 'Get out of my car.' Mike got out, slammed the door shut, and walked over to Amber."

"When the light turned green, I hit the gas. I was so scared that I didn't know what to do. Amber meant business. She didn't make idle threats. She was going to give me a real beating and who knows what else. There was no doubt in my mind about that. I kept thinking, *If I can just get out of here before they get home, they'll be gone by the time I get home from work.*"

"My body was shaking. I kept asking myself, *What just happened? What just happened?* I was almost in shock. I stepped on the gas and got home as fast as I could. When I parked the car, I saw Amber's purse in the floorboard behind my seat. My heart almost stopped beating. I didn't want her to have any excuse to come over to my house, so I picked up her purse, ran to their house, tossed it on the front porch, ran back to my house, went inside, and locked the front door. I thought, *I'm okay now. I'm inside my house."*

"I wanted to call Justin and tell him what happened, but I couldn't find the phone. Frantically, I hit the page button and heard the phone beeping in the bedroom so I ran to get it. It was on Justin's dresser next to a .45 pistol. I moved the pistol about 15 feet, from the bedroom to the corner of our entertainment center in the living room."

Justin has two .45 caliber semiautomatic pistols. Cyndi had gone with him to fire one of them, but she had never fired the pistol on his dresser that morning. It's fair to say that Cyndi wasn't proficient with weapons. For instance, she knew how to pull back the slide to chamber a round, but until that day, she had never actually done it without Justin's help.

"I called Justin and told him the whole story. I said, 'Amber's serious about beating me up. She'll be over here in a few minutes. I don't know what to do, and I have to go to work. Do you think I should call your mom and ask her to come over here and sit with me while I get ready?' I was afraid Amber would break into the house while I was in the shower and attack me. There's no telling what she'll do when she gets angry. I even thought she might destroy my car in the driveway. Anything was possible."

****

"Why call Justin?" I asked. "Why not call the police instead?" Those are easy questions to ask in the safety of my living room with no one outside threatening me. But if you're 22 years old and you have no experience whatsoever with law enforcement authorities, calling the police isn't the first thing that pops into your head. Besides, Cyndi didn't want to get Amber into any trouble, especially on her last day in town. She believed Amber would be on the bus in a few hours so why make an issue out of something as ridiculous as torn window tinting. All Cyndi needed to do was take a shower and leave for work, or so she thought.

Maybe Cyndi should have known intuitively to call the police, but is it really that obvious? Maybe her parents should have told her about situations like this. Then she would have been prepared. I suppose we could try to shift the blame to them, but did you tell your children? I didn't tell mine. Maybe Justin should have called the police. Why did he call his mother instead? And why didn't Justin's mother call the police? She's an adult. These are all great questions in theory, but Cyndi faced an immediate threat. There wasn't a lot of time to contemplate theoretical possibilities.

Sitting in a comfortable chair with no pressure and time to think, it's easy to criticize, but the truth is that you don't know what you would have done in that situation, either. This isn't the kind of thing that most of us think about, and it's not something we go over with our children. But I can tell you this. My daughters will read this book.

"Of course, I would call the police today," Cyndi said, "but that never even entered my mind. I turned to Justin for help. I thought his mother's presence would be enough."

****

"Out of the blue, I thought about my dog. It occurred to me that Amber might kill my dog. I wouldn't put it past her. Amber and Mike lived in Maryland with some people named Tiffany and Aaron before they moved to South Carolina. One night they were sitting in our living room, and they told us that they got into a fight with Tiffany and Aaron just before they left. Out of spite or vengeance or something, Amber and Mike decided to leave them a little message."

"They placed needles and syringes around the house so it would look like both of them were shooting up drugs. That was designed to create tension between Tiffany and Aaron as a farewell gift. That's the way Amber was. Then she bragged about stealing Tiffany's clothes and other things. They even took their toilet paper. Can you imagine that? If they did those things to their *friends* in Maryland, what might they try to do to me? I didn't know. Justin said he would call his mother and ask her to come over. Like I said, I thought that would be enough."

****

"I took the fastest shower I've ever taken in my life, got dressed, and was drying my hair with a towel when I heard a loud pounding on my front door. Needless to say, I didn't get away before Amber and Mike got home."

BAM, BAM, BAM, BAM, BAM.

"Amber was beating on my front door again...hard, very hard, much harder than the first time."

"My heart almost stopped beating. I was so scared that I could hardly breathe. I stood completely still and didn't make a sound. I didn't even think about opening the door. Then she started hammering on the door again. The sound of it was terrifying because I knew that if she came inside my house she would be pounding on me."

BAM, BAM, BAM, BAM, BAM.

"Finally the pounding stopped, and I waited long enough for Amber to get home. Then I tiptoed silently to the front door and looked out of the peep hole. I was scared that I would see Amber's eye on the other side looking back at me, but I didn't. All I could see was the front porch, the front yard, and the street in front of our house. It was like looking through a tunnel."

"Slowly, I unlocked the front door and opened it. I was as careful as I could be, because I didn't want to make a sound. When the front door opened, it created a suction that pulled the storm door shut and made a rattling noise. I opened the door, leaned out, and saw Amber walking toward their house."

"Amber must have heard the storm door rattle so she looked over her shoulder and made eye contact with me. That was all it took. She turned around immediately and started walking back toward my house. Then she started shouting at me."

"By then, I was standing on my doormat with a towel wrapped around my head holding the storm door close to my body. Amber kept coming toward me. It was a threatening pace, and she never stopped screaming at me the whole time."

"You talk a lot of shit, don't you?" Amber said. "We're going to settle this shit right now."

"'I'm not going to fight you,' I said. Fighting Amber would have been ridiculous. She weighed at least 100 pounds more than me. It would have been like Rocky Balboa fighting Dakota Fanning, preposterous. Plus, she was pregnant. Still, Amber wanted to fight. She was marching toward me and hollering, 'We're going to settle this shit right now.'"

"I said it again. 'I'm not going to fight you. You just need to go home and everything will be fine.'"

"No. Fuck that. We're going to settle this shit right now," Amber yelled at the top of her lungs as she kept coming closer and getting louder by the second.

"I'm not going to fight you Amber. Go home. It's my car, and I'm not mad. I can't understand why you're mad."

"I don't think we tore your tint."

"It doesn't matter. I'm not mad. It's okay."

"It's not okay," Amber screamed. "We're going to settle this shit right now. Come on out bitch. Come on out."

"She was taunting me, but I wasn't going to fight her. When she got to the steps and climbed up on the porch, I went inside the house, closed the storm door, and fumbled around trying to lock it. I was so scared that my whole body was shaking, and I was having trouble sliding the lock into place. Finally, I got the lock to slide in about halfway, but it wasn't totally secure."

"The only thing between Amber's face and mine was that flimsy glass storm door. Her face was red and covered with sweat. She was squinting her eyes and yelling at me, 'If you don't come out right now, I'm coming in there and I'll drag your sorry ass out.' I was looking directly into her eyes. I've never seen such hate in all of my life."

"Amber grabbed the storm door handle, and started yanking on it as hard as she could. She was screaming like a person who had lost control. 'Let me in. Let me in. Let me in.' By that time, my neighbors had started coming out of their houses to watch the spectacle. I was scared and embarrassed."

"The third time she jerked the storm door handle, I heard a loud POP. The lock gave way; the door flew open; and Amber was inside my house stomping toward me. Her shoulders were raised, and her hands were balled up tightly into fists. I backed up as fast as I could. Suddenly, I was leaning against the entertainment center. I don't know why I didn't close and lock the wood door. I was so scared that I just wasn't thinking clearly."

"I picked up the pistol, threw off the holster, cocked it, and said, 'Go home Amber. Everything will be fine. Just go home. I'm not going to fight you. Just go home.' I was pleading with her, begging her, but it didn't do any good. She just kept coming toward me, closer and closer."

"When I pointed the gun at her, she sneered at me and mockingly said, 'You've got a fucking gun. Are you going to fucking shoot me? Fuck you bitch.'"

"I didn't know what to do. I was scared, and she kept getting closer. When she was right on top of me, I mean inches away from me, I turned my head and closed my eyes. The pistol just went off. I didn't mean to pull the trigger. I heard the sound, felt the gun push against my hand, and opened my eyes. Amber was falling to the floor. She fell straight down. She just collapsed to her knees and fell backwards. When I saw that, I started crying and screaming, 'Oh God. Oh God. Oh God.'"

****

"Mike was at my house in a few seconds. He grabbed Amber under her arms and pulled her straight back to lay her down flat. Then he started screaming at me, 'You shot her. You shot her. You fucking shot her.'"

"I was looking for the phone to call 911, but I couldn't find it. Then I found it on the kitchen table and called. I said, 'I just shot someone coming into my house.'"

"Mike was still screaming at me. I gave him the towel that was wrapped around my head and told him to stop the bleeding. I was afraid he was going to come in after me, and I was still shaking. I was walking back and forth with the phone in one hand and the pistol in the other. Mike was trying to do CPR, but he didn't know how to do it. He was just beating on Amber's stomach."

"Amber was about 4 feet inside my house when I shot her. When Mike stretched her out, her feet were on the threshold of my front door, but her head was on the porch."

****

An ambulance arrived within minutes. The medical crew had to wait down the street until police officers secured the scene. According to the Anderson County Sheriff's Office Crime Scene Log, September 8, 2006, case number 2006-32582, at 9:45 a.m. Deputy Craig Holbrooks arrived. He stepped over Amber's body, came into Cyndi's house, and handcuffed her behind her back.

Deputy Holbrooks' first question to Cyndi was "Where's the gun?" By that time, she had placed the pistol on the kitchen table. Deputy Holbrooks took the gun and Cyndi outside to his car. He tossed the gun in the front seat and put Cyndi in the backseat.

At about that time, Detective William Vaughn arrived. He happened to be nearby when he heard the call from dispatch, and he was the first detective at the scene. He sat in the backseat of Deputy Holbrooks' car with Cyndi. It was a hot morning, and inside the car was stifling. Cyndi was having an anxiety attack; she was sweating profusely; and her breathing was strained. The detective took Cyndi to his car where it was cooler, placed her in the front seat, and handcuffed her with her hands in front so she could breathe more freely. Then he took her statement.

Cyndi was a 22-year-old woman who had never been in trouble with law enforcement officials, much less been considered a suspect in a homicide investigation. Minutes before Detective Vaughn's arrival, Cyndi had been through the most horrific ordeal in her life, a terrifying experience that few of us will ever encounter. She was scared out of her senses.

Under those conditions, it's a miracle that she could string words together in sentences and give the detective a coherent statement, but her natural instinct was to cooperate fully with him because she had nothing to hide. In fact, she wanted him to know what happened. At that moment, Detective Vaughn knew only two things. A woman had been shot, and Cyndi Marchbanks was the shooter. Those facts were never in doubt.

Although Cyndi tried to give the detective all the relevant facts, she didn't tell him everything and he misunderstood some of the things she said. They were minor misunderstandings, but they were misunderstandings nonetheless. She wasn't intentionally trying to withhold information, to mislead him, or to confuse him. Under those trying circumstances, she simply couldn't recall every detail and present them in an orderly way. That should come as no surprise.

Detective Vaughn wrote down what Cyndi told him in his words. When he finished taking her statement, he asked her to read and sign what he wrote. It was the Anderson County Sheriff's Office Advisory of Rights form.

Dutifully, Cyndi complied with his request. In her state of mind, she did little more than glance at the document before signing it. After she signed the statement, Detective Vaughn gave Cyndi a piece of paper with her Miranda rights written on it. According to Sheriff's Office records, she read her rights and initialed the document at 10:11 a.m. That was about 40 minutes after the shooting and 25 minutes after Detective Vaughn's arrival at the scene.

Chapter 4
They're Going to Charge You with Murder

Cyndi leaned back in her chair, folded her hands, shook her head, took a deep breath, and said, "While I was sitting in Detective Vaughn's car giving him my statement, I kept asking him when they would know if Amber was okay, and he kept saying, 'I don't know. I don't know.' That's all he said. I kept thinking, *She'll be okay*, but I was wrong."

Actually, Detective Vaughn did know. According to the South Carolina Law Enforcement Division, Forensic Services Laboratory Report by Edward A. Porter, Forensic Specialist, October 4, 2007, SLED LAB: L07-06698, p. 3, the bullet entered Amber's body through her chin and pierced her spinal cord. She died almost instantly. This is how Dr. Brett Woodard, the pathologist who performed Amber's autopsy, explained it:

> "...the victim (Amber Robey) suffered a brain shot with the bullet severing the victim's spinal cord....this trauma would have immediately incapacitated the victim, making the victim unable to move her arms and legs....the victim fell down immediately, with gravity, once she was shot, and did not make any further movements."

As soon as Cyndi initialed the Miranda document, Detective Vaughn said, "Let's take a ride." Cyndi didn't have a clue where they were going. She thought that he must be taking her to a quiet place to ask her more questions. That seemed to make sense because of the constant interruptions at the scene of the shooting. But Detective Vaughn already knew that Cyndi was being charged with murder. He just didn't tell her.

Detective Vaughn was very cooperative when I talked with him in the spring of 2008. He did his best to help me understand exactly what happened at the scene of the shooting from his perspective. But his involvement that day was limited, so he had to stop short of telling me why Cyndi was charged with murder less than 2 hours after the shooting and before all the facts were gathered and examined thoroughly. That was the most important question I had then, and as far as I'm concerned, it remains unanswered to this day.

Repeatedly Detective Vaughn said, "I know why she was charged with murder at the scene, but I can't discuss it with you. You'll have to get that information from Detective Matheson. He can tell you if he wants to. He was in charge of the investigation, and he's the person who made the decision to charge Cyndi with murder."

****

Cyndi wiped a tear from her eye. "There was a lot of activity at my house with police, the ambulance crew, and media people milling around. More people kept arriving every minute. Detective Vaughn drove me to the Anderson County Detention Center—ACDC. Along the way, I continued to ask him, 'Is Amber okay? Do they know anything yet?' He kept saying, 'I don't know.'"

"When we drove up to ACDC, I had no idea where we were. I didn't even know it was there. ACDC has an intimidating appearance. There are fences and rolls of barbed wire and razor wire everywhere. The foul odor inside that place hit me in the face like a sledge hammer. I hate that putrid chemical smell. Today, I get sick at my stomach whenever I get a whiff of that stench. It doesn't matter where I am. I associate that smell with the time I spent at ACDC locked up like a caged animal."

****

The first order of business upon arrival at ACDC was check in, only Cyndi didn't know it was check in. "When we went inside, they started asking me a lot of questions...things like 'do you have any allergies?' That seemed strange to me, but I didn't mind. I told them everything they wanted to know. I thought about telling them that I was there only to talk with Detective Vaughn. I'm sure they would have gotten a kick out of that."

Cyndi smiled and shook her head. "I had no idea that I was being incarcerated. That never even entered my mind. Why would it? I had nothing to hide. I hadn't done anything wrong. All I did was defend myself inside my own home. There was absolutely no reason for me to think that I was being thrown into jail. I expected to be home that afternoon. Instead, I was about to be locked up with crackheads and murderers and drug addicts and thieves."

The reality of Cyndi's situation started to sink in when Detective Vaughn handed her an orange jump suit and flip-flops and told her to put them on. "They said I could keep my bra if it didn't have underwire. If it had underwire, they said they would have to remove it. That's when I knew that my life was about to change."

Dressed out in her new attire, Cyndi was placed in a holding cell. Within minutes, Detective Vaughn came in and said, "Amber didn't make it. They're going to charge you with murder."

"*Murder.* That word terrifies me. It's hard to describe how I felt. It was like being hit by a bolt of lightning. Amber was dead, and I was being charged with *murder.* I was almost numb. Thoughts started racing through my mind. *How can that be? She broke into my house. What should I have done, let her kill me? I didn't want to hurt Amber. I begged her to leave. I was trying to help her. In fact, I was the only one trying to help her. Something's wrong here.* My legs gave out, and I collapsed to the floor. I couldn't even talk."

****

According to the Sheriff's Office Crime Scene Log dated September 8, 2006, the chief detective for Cyndi's case, Kevin Matheson, arrived at the scene at 10:29 a.m. That's about an hour after the shooting. During a telephone interview in the spring of 2009, Detective Matheson told me that he arrived earlier than that, but he was outside Cyndi's house meeting with other detectives to make sure the investigation was moving along properly.

According to a Sheriff's Office supplemental report dated February 19, 2007, Detective Matheson reviewed Cyndi's and Mike's statements, surveyed the scene, and instructed several detectives to canvass the neighborhood and interview witnesses. He also sent a detective to EZ Pawn.

The Incident Report filed by Deputy Holbrooks says that the time of arrest was 12:10 p.m., but that can't be correct. Here's why. The Receiving Screening Form at the Anderson County Detention Center says that Cyndi arrived at 11:50 a.m., and Detective Vaughn told me explicitly that Detective Matheson charged Cyndi with murder before he left the scene.

I drove from Cyndi's house to ACDC three times to see how long it takes. Maintaining the speed limit, it took me more than 20 minutes each time so I'll assume that Detective Vaughn was able to complete the trip in just 20 minutes. That means Detective Matheson charged Cyndi with murder by 11:30 a.m. at the very latest. That's just 2 hours after the shooting and about 1 hour and 45 minutes after the first officer arrived at the scene. This is a critical point. The entire investigation from start to finish was completed in less than 2 hours.

Is that important? I think it is, but you be the judge. Let's begin by fleshing out the scenario:

- Detective Matheson arrived at the scene. The report says that it's 10:29 a.m., or about an hour after the shooting, but the detective says he arrived earlier than that. The shooting took place at about 9:30 a.m., so let's assume he arrived at that time and started the investigation immediately. Keep in mind that according to the Anderson County Sheriff's Office Crime Scene Log, the first officer to actually reach the scene was Deputy Craig Holbrooks, and he arrived at 9:45 a.m.

- The first thing Detective Matheson did was look around the house for a few minutes to familiarize himself with the situation. He found out what had been done already, and he talked briefly with the officers who were involved in the investigation. I know for a fact that he talked with Detective Vaughn for several minutes about Cyndi and her statement.

- Detective Matheson called his team together, or he talked with them individually which takes more time, and gave them instructions.

- The detectives spread out and visited Cyndi's neighbors to get their statements.

- Detective Matheson dispatched an officer to EZ Pawn to gather information while he remained at the scene examining Cyndi's and Mike's statements, among other things.

- In due course, the officers completed their assigned tasks and returned to the scene.

- Detective Matheson pieced together the information they collected, analyzed the data, and called the Solicitor's Office. In the end, he concluded that Cyndi committed murder, and it wasn't even 11:30 a.m. Less than 2 hours had elapsed since the shooting, and the investigation was over.

This depiction may not be accurate in every detail, but it has to be fairly close to what actually happened. Was Detective Matheson's decision to charge Cyndi with murder premature? Again, you be the judge.

I've driven from Cyndi's house to EZ Pawn and back. That round trip takes at least 15 to 20 minutes with virtually no traffic even if you don't get out of the car to talk with anyone. If you take the time to go inside and question a potential witness, it takes longer than that, much longer.

The woman from EZ Pawn who purchased the television set from Mike and Amber told me that the detective who interviewed her was inside the store for at least 45 minutes so I know that part of the investigation took more than an hour. That was the least complicated part of the investigation because the woman at EZ Pawn had no knowledge about the shooting incident. All she could contribute to the investigation was information about the television set and her opinion about Mike's and Amber's demeanor while they were inside the store for a matter of minutes.

I realize that the detectives gathered information simultaneously, but when they returned to the scene of the shooting to report their findings to Detective Matheson, they did it individually. Detective Matheson had to read the hand-written reports the detectives prepared while they interviewed witnesses and/or he talked with them about the information they gathered. Then he talked with someone in the Solicitor's Office, probably the solicitor. How much detail did the detective share with her? What did she tell him? How long did that call take? These are important questions because at the end of that conversation Detective Matheson charged Cyndi with murder.

In my scenario, I tried to give Detective Matheson every benefit of the doubt. For instance, I assumed that there were 2 hours of investigation, but as you know, in reality the investigation could have lasted no longer than 1 hour and 45 minutes. I also allowed no time for small talk or for casual comments, but let's be clear about this fact. Detectives are human, and this case was not your run-of-the-mill shooting incident.

You can bet that there was some bantering back and forth among the detectives at the scene of the shooting and probably some snide remarks as well. It's unrealistic to believe that those kinds of things did not take place. How much time was wasted in that manner? I can only guess, but keep in mind that we're racing against the clock here. We have less than 120 minutes to gather all the facts, examine the evidence, discuss the situation thoroughly, confer with the solicitor, and make an informed decision, so every second counts.

****

In the Sheriff's Office supplemental report dated February 19, 2007 that I mentioned earlier, Detective Matheson explained why he charged Cyndi with murder at the scene:

> "After reviewing the statements obtained from witnesses on scene as well as the statement from the defendant herself, I found overwhelming evidence to support the listed charges. Marchbanks had several opportunities to call Law Enforcement from the safety of her home. Marchbanks indicated that she was behind a locked door with the victim walking away from her residence after she armed herself with a firearm. At that time, Marchbanks was in no danger what so ever (sic) and in fact, the altercation appeared to be over all together. Marchbanks (sic) decision to unlock the door and confront Robey while armed with a firearm clearly shows that she was not in a position that gave her no choice but to defend herself. Marchbanks had several options at this point other than unlocking the door and confronting Robey. At that time, I instructed that Marchbanks be transported to the Anderson County Detention Center and held for the charge of murder."

It is clear from this report that Cyndi's calling Justin instead of the police had a lot to do with Detective Matheson's decision to charge her with murder, and that's exactly what he told me when I talked with him in early 2009. According to the detective, Cyndi was inside her house with the door shut and locked. To him, it made perfect sense that she should have called the police if she anticipated any problems.

Should Cyndi have called the police? Yes, without a doubt, and she admits that not calling them was a mistake. Even so, failing to call the police is not a crime. It certainly isn't grounds for a murder charge. I've already explained why calling the police wasn't the first thing on Cyndi's mind that morning.

This is the all important question. Did Detective Matheson actually have "overwhelming evidence" to support a murder charge as he stated in the report? I don't think so, but I don't want to jump too far ahead at this point. I will simply say this. At the very least, the detective's report leaves plenty of room for doubt, and reasonable doubt is all the law requires for an acquittal in a murder case.

For example, opening the front door to her home may not have been a wise thing for Cyndi to do, but was it illegal? Absolutely not, and Cyndi certainly did not intend to provoke a fight. She was scared senseless. Still, she knew that in a matter of minutes she would have to walk to her car and drive to work. From Cyndi's perspective, what was wrong with checking to see if Amber was gone? And what about the loaded pistol? It was there for protection. Owning a gun isn't a crime in South Carolina and neither is using one to defend yourself. Besides, it was Justin's pistol.

This is the point. Saying that you have "overwhelming evidence" does not mean that you actually have it, but this much is certain. Overwhelming evidence is required to obtain a murder conviction.

In my conversation with Detective Matheson, he repeated this summation of the facts a number of times:

- Cyndi was inside her home;
- the door was shut and locked;
- she was safe;
- she had time to call Justin and take a shower, but she didn't have time to call 911;
- she opened the door after Amber walked away from the porch; and
- she had a loaded pistol in the house;
- and she was ready to use it.

The detective is right about those facts, as far as they go, but as I've pointed out already, they do not constitute "overwhelming evidence" of murder.

****

Below is a complete list of the information Detective Matheson had at his disposal when he charged Cyndi with murder:

1) Cyndi's statement,
2) Deputy Holbrooks' observations upon arrival,
3) Mike Jackson's statement, the one he gave on the day of the shooting,
4) brief statements from Cyndi's neighbors that were gathered by the detectives,
5) information from EZ Pawn, and
6) information from the solicitor.

At this stage of my analysis, I don't want to go into detail examining the evidence, but I do want to bring up a few important points that will help you to understand what transpired at the scene of the shooting. Cyndi claimed self-defense in her statement to Detective Vaughn, and we know that Detective Matheson reviewed her statement. According to South Carolina law, when a person claims self-defense the burden of proof is on the prosecutor. She must prove beyond any reasonable doubt that it wasn't self-defense. Keep that fact in mind. I'll deal with it in more detail later because it should have influenced the detective's and the solicitor's thinking.

On the day of the shooting, Mike Jackson told Detective McBride that Cyndi shot Amber because she was angry about the torn window tint. According to him, there was no other motive for the shooting. Detective Matheson must have believed him. We know that the solicitor believed him because that was the theory of the case Assistant Solicitor Catherine Huey presented in court in October 2007, more than a year after the shooting. Mike Jackson was the one and only source for that piece of information.

But Mike Jackson didn't actually see the shooting. According to his statement and Cyndi's statement, he was inside his house, and he ran over to Cyndi's house after he heard the gunshot. So, is he a reliable witness in this case? Even more to the point, is his testimony alone sufficient to win a guilty verdict? Deputy Holbrooks didn't witness the shooting either. He saw only the aftermath, so his statement was neutral. Later, you'll see excerpts from the eyewitness testimony provided by Cyndi's neighbors. All of them supported her statement.

****

When all is said and done, we know one thing for certain. Detective Matheson did not have enough evidence to meet the beyond a reasonable doubt standard of proof because Cyndi was acquitted by a jury of her peers. But the trial took place more than a year after the shooting so this is the pertinent question. On the day of the shooting, or more precisely within 2 hours of the shooting, was their reasonable doubt?

Mike Jackson's statement left plenty of room for doubt. That fact will become obvious later. At most, Detective Matheson had probable cause to charge Cyndi with murder, and even that is questionable. The probable cause standard is satisfied when these conditions are met:

1. The facts and circumstances at that time (i.e., before an exhaustive investigation and examination) could lead a reasonable person to conclude that a murder had been committed.
2. The facts and circumstances at that time could lead a reasonable person to believe that Cyndi committed the murder.

You can make an argument, a weak one, that Mike Jackson's statement satisfied those criteria. Detective Matheson had no other data that even comes close to looking like evidence that Cyndi Marchbanks murdered Amber Robey. That fact will become obvious later when you read her neighbors' statements.

45

Under normal conditions it's foolish to use a probable cause standard for a murder charge because the facts and circumstances that lead one reasonable person to believe a murder occurred could just as easily lead another reasonable person to believe that it was self-defense. It might make sense for a police officer to charge a notorious gang leader with murder based on probable cause simply to get him off the streets for a while. Likewise, it might serve the community's interests to arrest a suspected serial rapist and put him behind bars based on nothing more than probable cause before completing a thorough investigation. Cyndi Marchbanks was not and is not a threat to the community, nor was she a flight risk.

Undoubtedly, some people will argue that I'm just Monday morning quarterbacking, but let me assure you that I am not. I'm simply taking an objective look at the evidence and trying to make sense of what happened. I'm completely ignoring the fact that we have a high-profile case on our hands and a solicitor who is facing a re-election campaign. You can rest assured that political careers are launched and/or rehabilitated on the backs of cases like this one. They don't come along every day, either.

The solicitor was about to face a tough opponent in her re-election bid. Did that influence the decision to charge Cyndi with murder and/or the decision not to drop the charges against her when other evidence came to light? Whatever the case may be, there can be no denying this fact. Prosecutors have been known to pursue serious charges in high profile cases for entirely political reasons. Is this case an example of that kind of abuse? I'll let the evidence speak for itself.

Law enforcement authorities had to know from the moment the first detective arrived at the scene that they would be inundated with media coverage. Just look at the facts:

- A pregnant woman was shot in the face.
- She died and the child was delivered postmortem via Caesarean section.

- The odds of the baby surviving were practically nil.

This is high drama. It's riveting. It's the kind of thing that makes people buy newspapers and watch the evening news. If there ever was a case that would captivate people's attention, this was it. Did that topic come up when Detective Matheson talked with the solicitor? Did she ask him how many media people were at the scene? Exactly what did she tell Detective Matheson?

****

Before I go any further, I need to point out that taking Cyndi's statement without giving her the Miranda warning violated her constitutional rights. Detective Vaughn would have been under no obligation to read Cyndi her rights if she had been free to go. However, she wasn't able to leave on her own volition because she was handcuffed and locked up inside a police vehicle.

That critical error never became an issue because Cyndi did a very good job of conveying the facts to Detective Vaughn, and he did a commendable job of writing down what she told him. Had there been a problem, though, Cyndi's lawyer, Druanne White, could have had her statement thrown out. About that fact, there can be no doubt.

Now, think about these circumstances. Under excruciating conditions, within minutes of the shooting, handcuffed inside a police vehicle, short of breath, sweating profusely, on the verge of going into shock, and with absolutely no knowledge about South Carolina's laws pertaining to murder, self-defense, and defense of habitation—all of which were pertinent in this case—Cyndi Marchbanks laid out the facts for Detective Vaughn correctly the first and only time she was asked. If she had wanted to lie or to present a "favorable view" of the shooting from her perspective, she wouldn't have known what to say. The only so-called "problems" with her statement were caused by misunderstandings, and they were minor.

Neither Detective Matheson nor the solicitor gave that vital information any credence at all. Instead, they grabbed onto Mike Jackson's statement as though it was as good as gold, ran with it, and never looked back. They must have thought that it was solid enough to charge Cyndi with murder.

Later, I will discuss a second statement that Mike Jackson gave to Detective Matheson on October 19, 2006, and I'll compare it with the one he gave at the scene of the shooting. For now, just let it suffice to say that both of his statements are seriously flawed. That fact should have been obvious on the day of the shooting, but it was painfully clear when Mike gave his second statement a few weeks later. That was more than a year before Cyndi's trail.

****

The decision to charge Cyndi Marchbanks with murder set in motion Anderson County's law enforcement apparatus. From that moment forward, law enforcement officials had two primary objectives:

1. to convict Cyndi Marchbanks of murder and
2. to justify the decision to charge her with murder in the first place.

Despite the presumption of innocence, most citizens believe that people who are accused of crimes are guilty. Once the Anderson community bought into the notion that Cyndi Marchbanks murdered a mother and her unborn child, dismissing the charges against her became a very complicated issue.

The solicitor is the last line of defense against injustice. In this case, that person is Chrissy Adams, the Solicitor in South Carolina's 10th Judicial Circuit. As the duly elected official responsible for prosecuting suspected criminals, she has the constitutional authority and the sworn duty to investigate all charges thoroughly, to collect and examine all the facts, and to drop charges if there is sufficient exculpatory evidence and/or insufficient evidence for conviction. In the final analysis, she is the person responsible for determining how a case is handled.

Chapter 5

I Think I Can Get You 10 Years
on a Plea Deal

"My grandmother called the authorities to make sure I had an attorney, so they sent one to meet with me on the day I arrived at ACDC. His name is John J. Stathakis. I don't think he wanted to have anything to do with me. He acted like he was assigned the case...like he was next in line to represent a deadbeat and he wanted to get it over with as quickly as possible. He asked me what happened, and when I started giving him the facts, he began saying things like 'This is not good' and 'That's not going to work.' The next day, Mr. Stathakis told my mother that he thought he could plea my sentence down to 10 years in prison. Without any hesitation, my mother said, 'NO WAY!'"

"Justin's mother, Gail, told me that I should hire Druanne White as my lawyer. Gail worked for her while Druanne was the solicitor. Gail said, 'She's the best.' Druanne came over to ACDC on Saturday morning to meet with me. After we met, she shut down her office and took her staff to canvass my neighborhood. They met with all of my neighbors, took pictures, and other things. I just wish she had been there on Friday immediately after the shooting. By Saturday morning, 50 million people had been in and out of my house touching things. I also wish I could have called Druanne before Detective Vaughn took my statement. She would have come down there right then. I'm positive things would have worked out differently if she had been there."

****

In the previous chapter, I said that they put Cyndi in a holding cell. That's a misnomer. That holding cell would become Cyndi's home for the next four days. The instant Cyndi's mother learned about her daughter's predicament, she came down from Maryland. She was at ACDC first thing Saturday morning making sure Cyndi had everything she needed…clean underwear in particular.

"They told my mother that they would issue me underwear, but they didn't. I wore the same pair of underwear for the first 7 days I was in jail." Cyndi started laughing as she shook her head. "I wasn't allowed to take a shower until the fourth day. Thankfully, they gave me a tiny bar of soap, a little toothbrush, and a small tube of toothpaste. When I finally did take a shower, I smelled awful."

Altogether, Cyndi spent 34 days in jail. Her first stay in jail lasted 14 days. It started on the day of the shooting and ended with her release on bond. When Amber's baby, Hailey, died about three weeks later, she spent another 20 days in jail. "The second time I went to jail, I checked in wearing 6 pairs of underwear. I was determined not to have another underwear problem."

"When Hailey died, I was charged with a second count of murder. My case was already high-profile, but Hailey's death generated another round of intense media attention. People who thought I was a monster after Amber's death probably thought I was a hideous fiend after Hailey's death. I think the solicitor, Chrissy Adams, wanted to show the community how tough she was. Since I was out of jail on bond for the first murder charge, Hailey's death gave her another opportunity to make me spend some time in jail. She allowed me to turn myself in rather than sending police officers out to re-arrest me, but she purposely chose a time for me to turn myself in when court wouldn't be in session so I would have to spend at least a couple of weeks in jail."

****

"The accommodations at ACDC aren't inviting to say the least," Cyndi said as she shook her head. "There are no beds and no pillows. You sleep on a mat that's placed inside a heavy plastic thing that looks like a small boat."

"When I was in jail the first time, I had no shampoo, no conditioner, and no other incidentals for almost a week because those things have to be ordered from the canteen at ACDC. Inmates place their orders and pay on Tuesday. The orders are delivered from Columbia [South Carolina] in a small bag on Thursday. This may sound strange, but I was thrilled when I got my first bag of incidentals. They were just simple things that I used to take for granted...things like shampoo and deodorant and conditioner. Can you imagine getting excited about deodorant or soap?"

"The food at ACDC isn't very good, so I didn't eat a lot. They wake you up at 6:00 in the morning for breakfast. A typical breakfast is plain oatmeal with scrambled eggs, but on Thursdays they served Cheerios with blueberry muffins. I ate breakfast on Thursdays. A typical lunch would be chicken nuggets with French fries. The French fries were always soggy because they were delivered in metal trays covered with foil. The condensation dripped all over the fries. For dinner, we had things like meatloaf, but the meat didn't seem to be cooked all the way through most of the time."

"One of my roommates would save some of her food and hide it in the cell. She ate it later as a snack. There are no refrigerators in the cells so you can imagine what it looked like by the time she ate it. I wanted to tell her that food poisoning is real. People get sick every day from contaminated food."

"Each cell has a stainless steel toilet with a sink on top. Some of the inmates washed their clothes in the toilet. I refused to do that. I washed my clothes in the sink. We hung our wet clothes up to dry in our cells on things that protruded from the walls. They weren't hooks, though. Nothing in the cells can be used to hurt yourself. Hooks aren't allowed."

"There's absolutely no privacy at ACDC. You go to the bathroom in front of people, and you take a shower in front of people. One black girl used to watch me every time I took a shower. The shower was directly across from her room, and there wasn't a shower curtain so there was nothing I could do about it. It was like taking a shower in front of a man. Finally, I had had enough. I looked at her and said, 'Haven't you ever seen a white girl naked before?' The other inmates said she was funny like that."

"During my first stay at ACDC, all the inmates were nice to me. They knew about my case, and they wanted me to give them information about the shooting. Druanne had told me not to talk with the other inmates about my case, so I didn't discuss it with anyone."

"If an inmate can get you to give her information on a high-profile case like mine, she can trade it to the solicitor for a reduction in her sentence. Several inmates constantly tried to pry information out of me. They weren't too subtle, either. I just brushed them off as best I could. Some of them made things up about me anyway and sent letters to the solicitor. I've got copies of the letters. They said things like 'she's not remorseful' or 'she doesn't care if the baby dies.' It was a bunch of lies, and none of it got into court because Druanne requested a polygraph test. They didn't stand a chance of passing a polygraph test."

****

When I spoke with Detective Matheson in early 2009, he told me that some inmates at ACDC volunteered evidence against Cyndi. The serious tone in his voice suggested that he thought I would be shocked by that revelation. It was as if he was sharing a closely guarded secret with me in confidence. According to the detective, Cyndi's fellow prisoners said she was nonchalant as she explained that she didn't care if the baby died and that she showed no signs of remorse.

It sounded as though the detective was telling me that those "facts" were proof that Cyndi was guilty of murder. I sensed a rapid change in his demeanor when I told him that I had read the letters inmates wrote to the solicitor. I explained that jailhouse snitches are notorious for trying to negotiate their sentences down by trading information that will help prosecutors convict high-profile suspects.

Nothing the inmates said had any bearing on the facts of the case, and their statements couldn't be corroborated or refuted by other information. At best, their so-called "evidence" was simply conjecture about Cyndi's state of mind. In a nutshell, it was worthless.

The detective insisted again that the inmates volunteered the information, as if that mattered. Since there was no quid pro quo, he was convinced that they were telling the truth. They were just being "good citizens," in a manner of speaking, who didn't expect anything in return.

It is an indisputable fact that the snitches' so-called "evidence" came to light more than 4 days after the shooting, so it had no bearing whatsoever on Detective Matheson's decision to file murder charges against Cyndi on the day of the shooting. It sounded to me as if he was trying to justify his decision. I thought, *He's more concerned about how he looks in all of this than he is about what happened to Cyndi.*

Eventually, I realized that we were getting nowhere, so I said, "Detective Matheson, the day after the shooting, Druanne White told Cyndi not to talk with the other inmates at ACDC about her case. She warned Cyndi to be careful because they would use anything she told them to help reduce their sentences."

That word of caution came 3 days before Cyndi met any other inmates. It's inconceivable to me that she would ignore Druanne's advice. She had nothing to gain and potentially a lot to lose by sharing information with other inmates—even trivial tidbits. Cyndi told me unequivocally that she did not talk with the other inmates about her case. I spent many hours meeting with Cyndi, and I know this: she is not an idiot.

I was surprised when the detective repeated his point yet again. The information the inmates provided was voluntary...and therefore accurate, he insisted. His dogged determination made me wonder if he really believed what he was telling me or if he was desperately clinging to any shred of so-called "evidence" that might support his decision to charge Cyndi with murder...no matter how improbable it was.

Next, Detective Matheson told me that the relationship between Cyndi and Justin and Amber and Mike was very open. He pointed out that Amber was in and out of Cyndi's house all the time. Of course, he was insinuating that when Amber entered Cyndi's house on the day of the shooting, it was not unusual in any way. In his mind, that was compelling evidence that Cyndi committed murder.

In general, Detective Matheson's assessment about the openness of the relationship between Cyndi and Amber is correct...as far as it goes. However, it fails to take into account these undeniable facts. On the morning of the shooting, Cyndi told Amber to go home, and she locked the door to keep Amber out of her house because Amber threatened to beat her to a pulp, or worse, before she left for work.

Those facts are crucial because they clearly indicate that the relationship changed. This is the essential question. Did Cyndi have the right to protect herself by ordering Amber not to enter her house given the fact that she had had an open door policy up until that time? Stated another way, was Cyndi obligated to maintain her open door policy with Amber even after Amber threatened to beat her up?

All things considered, I was taken aback by my discussion with Detective Matheson. It showed me that he is one strong-minded individual—some people might even say stubborn to a fault. I think it indicated that he has a hard time accepting facts that don't conform to his preconceived notions or admitting that there might be multiple ways to interpret the meaning of factual information. Worst of all, I think he has a problem admitting that he might be wrong. These are alarming proclivities, especially in law enforcement officials.

****

"This may sound strange," Cyndi said, "but there's one thing about being in jail that I'll always be thankful for. I had the time and the desire to pray and study the Bible. I read the Bible and prayed more in jail than I ever have in my life. The first time I was in jail, I read passages from the Bible that meant a lot to me. The second time, I read the entire New Testament plus Psalms and Proverbs. God really does work in mysterious ways. Mine wasn't a jailhouse conversion, but being in jail brought me to my knees. God got my attention. I'm grateful for that."

"I didn't want to hurt Amber's baby. She's the reason I asked Amber to come down here to start with. The first thing I did each morning was pray for Hailey, and I prayed for her constantly throughout the day until she died. I was so sorry I hurt her. I can't tell you how much I cried. I regret hurting Amber too, even though she intended to hurt me. I begged her to stop, pleaded with her to go home, but she just kept coming. Amber's mom and dad always treated me nicely. I didn't want to hurt them either. Every time I saw them in court, I couldn't help thinking, *I killed their daughter, my friend.* There's no question that I had a lot to pray about. My soul was aching. I was broken, and being in jail meant I had a lot of time to pray."

****

"When it finally hit me that Amber was really dead and that I had killed her, I started to sense her presence around me. That was very peculiar. I know it was just my imagination, but it was an eerie feeling all the same...as if Amber was there with me. I started having dreams too, bad dreams. I still have bad dreams, although not as often as I did at first."

"In one dream, I find Amber. She's not dead, but there's an area on her face that's blotted out. Since she isn't dead, I try to take her to my lawyer's office or to the police station or somewhere so people can see that she's still alive. In another dream, Amber sets me on fire. In another one, Amber ties me up and drives clothes hangers through my feet. Then she pulls out my toenails with pliers."

55

The worst of the bad dreams may be over, but Cyndi still has them. In one dream, Amber shoots Cyndi and stabs her. In another one, Amber is sitting in a room full of weapons of various sorts. While Cyndi watches, Amber sharpens a knife and looks at her menacingly. In this dream, Amber doesn't do anything. She just sits there sharpening the knife. In another dream, Amber chases Cyndi, catches her, and beats her to a pulp. Cyndi was correct when she said that Amber succeeded in transferring problems to her.

****

"Most of the guards at ACDC didn't treat me very well. While I was in the holding cell, they would come up to me and say things like, 'The girls are starting to ask about you. They want to know when we're going to bring you back.'"

"They were referring to the inmates who already had assigned cells. I didn't know what they were implying. I think they wanted to leave me wondering just to scare me. Finally, I asked one of them, 'What do you mean? Do they want to fight me?' She said, 'No. They just want to know when we're going to bring back the girl who killed that pregnant woman.' There's a TV in the permanent cell area. All of them had seen me on the news, and they knew that I was already in jail."

"There's a phone at ACDC that the prisoners can use. It's supposed to be turned on at 9:00 each morning. That phone was my lifeline. It was the only way I could make contact with the outside world, and I desperately wanted to talk with my family. I got up early each day to pray and read the Bible. By 10:00 or 10:30 when the phone was supposed to be on, I would say to the guard as nicely as I possibly could, 'I'm sorry to bother you, but when you have some time, would you please turn on the phone?'"

"They would give me one of two answers—'no' or 'is everybody up?' If someone else asked them to turn the phone on, they turned it on without any hesitation. To most of the guards, I was the little girl who killed the pregnant lady. When Hailey died, I became the baby killer. I was scum in most of their eyes. A couple of the guards were nice to me, though."

"The same thing happened with the TV. It was supposed to be turned on at 9:00 too. If I asked them to turn it on, they just ignored me, but if someone else asked them, on it came. It didn't matter one bit that I asked nicely. I wanted to tell them, 'I'm not a monster. I'm being punished for defending myself. Amber broke into my house to attack me. I begged her to leave, but she just kept coming. I didn't mean to shoot her, and I certainly didn't mean to kill her baby. Please don't judge me.' I didn't tell them, and I don't think it would have mattered anyway."

"They must have thought that I was some rich girl," Cyndi said as she started laughing. "Both of my parents work for Wal-Mart. I worked at O'Charley's as a waitress. We're not rich. My extended family put up land for my bond. Those guards didn't have any right to judge me or to treat me unfairly."

"Most of the guards liked to act tough. I think they wanted us to know that they were the good guys and we were the criminals. When I came back to ACDC the second time, I learned that while I was out on bond some of the guards had been taking bets on how much prison time I would get. My tragedy was fun and games for them. They shouldn't have done that."

"I'll never forget the night I was released from jail the first time. I had my bond hearing earlier that day, and I had to go back to jail after the hearing to do paperwork and clean up. Dinner was brought in while I was there. It was some kind of chili, but I didn't eat it. My parents told me that they would take me to Pizza Hut for dinner because I had a craving for a Supreme Pizza without onions."

"I was so excited about getting out of jail. I had everything bundled up and folded nice and neat. Then I had to sit there for four hours waiting to be released.   I fell asleep reading the Bible. · Someone woke me and said, 'Marchbanks, let's go.' Walking out of there was a great feeling. I was smiling and happy. I walked right past my family. I didn't even see them. I just kept walking. They had to grab my arm because I was heading out the front door."

****

"Sam Frazier, a deputy in the Sheriff's Office, escorted me to the courthouse on the day of my first bond hearing. I was wearing ankle bracelets, and my hands were handcuffed together and attached to a chain around my waist. Deputy Frazier called me a murderer that day, and he said, 'Some kind of friend you are.' What right did he have to say that? He didn't know me, and he didn't know anything about my case."

"I was trying to do everything Deputy Frazier told me to do, and he kept saying, 'Move it. Move it. Move it.' He sounded like a drill sergeant barking out orders. You can't walk very fast while you're wearing ankle bracelets. All of a sudden he said, 'Halt.' I thought he said, 'Haul,' so I tried to walk even faster. He didn't like that. With an angry tone he said, 'Yeah, keep walking. Just give me a reason to tase you.' He actually pulled out his taser, but I was trying to be obedient. It wasn't right for him to treat me like a convicted felon."

"The assistant solicitor at my first bond hearing, Mindy Hervey, told the judge that I was a danger to society and that I was a flight risk. She told him that if I did get out on bond, I needed to wear a GPS tracking device that costs something like $15 a day to use. Judge Nicholson looked at her and said, 'Why? If she had it on and she wanted to leave, all she would have to do is cut the band and leave it by the box. What good would it do for me to make her wear that thing?' He's the kind of judge we really need around here."

"I had a $100,000 surety bond. My extended family put up their land for the bond so I could get out of jail. I was so embarrassed at my bond hearing. I had to stand there in front of my whole family in my orange jump suit wearing shackles. You can't imagine what that feels like if you haven't done it."

****

"It's been more than a year since the shooting, but I still think about it. I'm not a mean, vindictive person. I didn't want to hurt Amber. I was guilty of one thing, though. I was guilty of trying to help a friend, but that's not a crime. I was foolish and immature too, but those aren't crimes either."

"Was it unreasonable for me to believe that I had a right to defend myself inside my own home? I don't think so. I was dumbfounded when Mr. Stathakis told my mother that he thought he could get me a 10 year sentence on a plea deal. My mother was angry, really angry. He made it sound like that was the best I could hope for…like I was definitely going to prison. The only question in his mind was how much jail time I would get.

He's a lawyer. He wanted to represent me, but without doing much of anything he was telling me I should expect to give up 10 years of my life for defending myself. I was really confused. I kept thinking, *Something is wrong here. This isn't justice. I'm being railroaded.* Was it ridiculous for me to expect a not guilty verdict if we went to trial? I hoped not, because that's what Druanne said we should do. I'm glad we followed her advice."

Chapter 6
Baby Hailey Dies

On September 8, 2006 at 9:45 a.m., about 15 minutes after the shooting, the emergency medical crew was allowed to begin its work. Amber Robey had no pulse, but there was Pulseless Electric Activity—PEA. PEA is sometimes referred to as Electromechanical Dissociation or Non-Perfusing Rhythm. It means that a heart rhythm was observed on an electrocardiogram.[1] There should have been a pulse, but there wasn't. For all practical purposes, Amber was dead.

Roughly 10 minutes later, Amber's body was in an ambulance heading for Anderson Area Medical Center (AnMed). She was asystole in route to AnMed. That means her heart wasn't contracting and pumping blood the way it's supposed to. Sometimes asystole is called "flatline." Amber was pronounced dead on arrival at AnMed at 10:03 a.m.

Emergency medical personnel at AnMed performed an ultrasound examination of Amber's womb. It revealed the baby's pulse. The medical staff sprung into action immediately, and Hailey Robey was delivered via Caesarean section on Amber's lifeless body. The baby was cyanotic (blue) at birth and apneic (not breathing). She had no spontaneous movement at delivery. Since blood flow to Amber's womb ended instantly when her heart stopped beating, Hailey had been deprived of oxygen for more than 30 minutes before she was born.

Hailey was placed under a warmer and given respiratory assistance by way of a breathing bag at 10:19 a.m. Compressions were initiated because her heart rate fell to 120 beats per minute (bpm), and she started having seizures. She was intubated at 10:21 a.m.

---

[1] http://www.answers.com/topic/electrocardiogram

The medical staff's work paid off. Hailey's heart rate increased to 148 bpm, and it eventually increased to 169 bpm. Her color went from blue to pink with 89 percent assisted respiration, and her body temperature stopped falling. It had dropped to 93.5 degrees at one point.

Suddenly, Hailey's heart rate started falling again so warm blankets were applied, and her heart rate jumped back up to 136 bpm. At about 11:00 a.m., she was transported to the Spartanburg (South Carolina) Regional Medical Center Neonatal Intensive Care Unit (NICU). According to Hailey's medical report, her condition upon discharge from AnMed was critical. At 11:15 a.m., Amber's body was transported to the morgue.

****

According to an article in *Circulation*, the Journal of the American Heart Association, "The best survival rate for infants >24 to 25 weeks in gestation occurs when the delivery of the infant occurs no more than 5 minutes after the mother's heart stops beating."[2] Emergency medical personnel didn't even begin CPR on Amber until more than 10 minutes after the shooting. Mike Jackson attempted to perform CPR before the medical crew arrived, but according to Cyndi, he didn't know how. That said, CPR helps, but it is no substitute for a functioning heart.

This is the awful truth. After Amber Robey's heart stopped beating, more than 10 minutes went by before skilled professionals performed CPR. More than 30 minutes passed between the time Amber's heart stopped beating and the time Hailey was delivered. Hailey entered this world oxygen starved and lifeless. She never took an unassisted breath. From the moment she was born, Hailey required life support, and she was on life support until the day she died.

Hailey never injured a living sole, and yet she was paying the price for the mistakes of others. The odds of Hailey surviving were almost zero regardless of

---

[2] http://circ.ahajournals.org/content/112/24_suppl/IV-150.full

what was done to help her. The likelihood that she would live a normal life was zero.

On October 18, 2006, 40 days after the shooting, Hailey Robey died. Anderson County Coroner Greg Shore ruled her death a homicide. Immediately, Cyndi was charged with a second count of murder, but the official cause of Hailey's death—the medical condition from which she actually died—was multisystem organ failure. That condition is common among premature infants of drug addicted mothers and newborn babies that have experienced oxygen deprivation. Hailey was fighting a losing battle from the moment she was born.

****

I was puzzled by the coroner's ruling. If Cyndi had been guilty of murdering Amber Robey, I would have understood why it made sense to charge her with a second count of murder when Hailey died, but at that point her case hadn't been adjudicated. She had merely been charged with a crime. Under our system of justice, a person is innocent until proven guilty. Cyndi's trial didn't take place until October 2007, more than a year after Hailey's death. It seemed logical to me that since the jury found Cyndi not guilty, Hailey's death could not have been a homicide.

I called Greg Shore and asked him about his ruling. His answer boiled down to this. Since Cyndi was accused of murdering Amber Robey, Hailey's death had to be a homicide. That means the coroner's ruling was based solely on the fact that Cyndi was charged with murder at the scene of the shooting less than two hours after the incident and before a thorough investigation and examination of the evidence.

I think the coroner became an innocent player in a senseless piling on of charges against Cyndi. One miscarriage of justice led to another which led to another, and on and on it went. The wheels of "justice" were in motion, and there was no stopping them. From the moment law enforcement officials made public accusations about Cyndi's guilt, they were reluctant to back off...even when they should have known that their evidence would not support any charge against her.

By the time Hailey died, it should have been clear that Cyndi acted in self-defense. If lingering doubt about her guilt remained, it should have been eliminated completely when Mike Jackson gave his second statement to Detective Matheson on October 19, 2006—the day following Hailey's death. Unfortunately, at that point I don't think the detective or the solicitor re-examined Mike's first statement—the one he gave on the day of the shooting. I don't think they could have, because if they had, they would have noticed serious discrepancies between his two versions of the facts. Those inconsistencies should have caused them to be hesitant about moving ahead with their case on the strength of his testimony.

****

The shooting of a pregnant woman is fodder for the media regardless of the circumstances. When a premature infant dies as a result of that shooting, the media has a field day. After Hailey Robey's death, Cyndi Marchbanks was portrayed in the media as an arch villain. Despite what actually happened, to many people in the Anderson community who knew only what they read in the newspaper or saw on television she became a heartless, cold-blooded killer.

Talking about Hailey's death was extremely difficult for Cyndi. I could tell that she felt responsible for Hailey's death even though she knew she acted in self-defense. In truth, Amber Robey's actions on September 8, 2006 led to her daughter's death. She broke into Cyndi's home intending to beat her to a pulp and who knows what else. Cyndi told Amber to leave, but she refused to go. When Cyndi aimed a loaded pistol at her, Amber mocked Cyndi and kept coming at her as if it didn't matter.

****

We were sitting in our living room the evening Cyndi discussed the shooting and Hailey's death. She was fighting back tears the whole time. It was difficult to watch. Then Cyndi turned her attention to the charges against her. "Druanne told me that she thought the chances were about 50/50 that I would be found not guilty regardless of the evidence because of the way people feel about babies. I was stunned...almost numb. I didn't do anything to hurt Hailey. I was trying to help her. She's the reason I wanted Amber to come down here. I wanted to help Amber get off of drugs so her baby would have a chance. I didn't want to hurt either of them."

Chapter 7
Let's Examine the Evidence

John Adams, our second president and one of our nation's Founding Fathers, said that ours is "a government of laws, and not of men." Thomas Paine, the author of *Common Sense* and one of the intellectual leaders of the American Revolution, said, "For as in absolute governments the king is law, so in free countries the law ought to be king; and there ought to be no other." For more than 2 centuries, men and women have fought and died to defend this principle. We are a nation governed by laws.

In our country, people should not be charged with crimes unless there is credible evidence that they broke the law. That's a fundamental tenet that distinguishes our nation from third world dictatorships that are governed according to the whims of petty tyrants. Keep that fact in mind as you read this chapter. If government agents are free to ignore our laws at their pleasure and attack any one of us, then all of us suffer.

****

These are the charges that were leveled against Cyndi by the prosecutor:

- Two counts of murder,
- death or injury to a child inutero, and
- two counts of possession of a deadly weapon during the commission of a violent crime.

Each murder charge and death or injury to a child inutero—three offenses—carried a penalty of 30 years to life with no chance for parole. That's a minimum of 90 years. The firearms violations, two of them, carried penalties of 5 years each with no chance for parole. That's a 10 year minimum. In total, Cyndi faced a 100-year minimum sentence with no chance for parole. She would be on trial to determine where she would spend the rest of her life.

****

As you already know, Cyndi claimed self-defense, and self-defense is a complete defense. That means the prosecutor had to prove beyond a reasonable doubt that Cyndi did not act in self-defense to win a guilty verdict. So this is the first question we need to think about. Did Cyndi act in self-defense? If the answer to that question is "yes," then for 14 months Cyndi and her family had to endure the agony of not knowing what might happen to her...and for no good reason. On top of that, the taxpayers of Anderson County South Carolina had to pony up for a pointless but expensive show trial.

We also need to consider this question. Was Cyndi Marchbanks Nifonged? Nifong is the last name of disgraced District Attorney Mike Nifong from Durham, North Carolina. He's the person responsible for pursuing the infamous case against several Duke University lacrosse players for allegedly gang raping a black female stripper.

You should recall that Nifong committed an array of offenses, some of them criminal, and was disbarred. On top of that, the good citizens of Durham, North Carolina had to shell out millions of dollars in damages to the exonerated lacrosse players. On August 31, 2007, Mike Nifong was found guilty of criminal contempt of court, sentenced to one day in jail, and fined $500. Subsequently, he was sued in civil court and filed for bankruptcy.

Nifonged is the past tense of the verb form of the disgraced prosecutor's last name. The use of that term suggests there was abundant exculpatory evidence in the case and that the evidence for conviction was either very weak or nonexistent, but the prosecutor went ahead with the case anyway for political reasons.

You be the judge. Was Cyndi Marchbanks Nifonged?

****

We'll begin our examination by taking a look at the law itself. The State of South Carolina provides protections for people who are attacked inside their homes. Those rights are laid out in the "Protection of Persons and Property Act." (See Appendix 1) This law recognizes the common law principle that a person's home is his castle. In a nutshell, it says that you have a right to protect yourself, your family, and others inside your home from intruders and attackers and to do it "without fear of prosecution or civil action."

The right to be safe inside your home is not a luxury reserved for the privileged few or for those deemed to be worthy at any given time according to the whims of law enforcement officials. According to the Act, if you are inside your home, you don't have to surrender your personal safety to anyone and you don't have to pull back or move away if someone invades your home. But the Act doesn't stop there. It goes on to say that you have a right to use deadly force against anyone who unlawfully and forcefully enters your home with the intent to inflict great bodily injury.

I'm not a lawyer, and I'm not giving legal advice. If you need legal help, hire an attorney. My sole purpose here is to present the South Carolina laws regarding self-defense and defense of habitation that applied in Cyndi's case. Below, I've identified the elements required to establish self-defense in a South Carolina legal proceeding as of the date of Cyndi's trial:

- You must be without fault in bringing on the difficulty. In other words, you can't provoke a fight, retreat into your home, and then claim self-defense when you have to defend yourself from an attack by the person you provoked.

- You were in imminent danger of death or serious bodily injury or you believed you were in danger of death or serious bodily injury.

- The court takes into account the physical condition and the characteristics of both the defendant and the victim, including size, age, and weight differences.

- You do not have to prove that you were actually in danger. You simply need to establish that you believed you were in imminent danger. In other words, you have the right to act on appearances even though you may be wrong.

- You had no other choice than to act as you did under those circumstances to avoid death or serious bodily injury.

- You are justified in using physical force if you believe it's the only way to prevent the unlawful use of physical force against you.

- You may use a degree of force that you believe is necessary to defend yourself from an unlawful use of force.

- You may use deadly physical force if you believe a lesser degree of force is inadequate, and you have reason to believe that you are in imminent danger of being killed or of sustaining great bodily injury.

- You have no duty to retreat inside your home even if you can do so safely.

According to South Carolina law, if a jury believes that you acted in self-defense, it must find you not guilty. It has no other choice. Even more, if there is reasonable doubt about whether you acted in self-defense, by law the jury must find you not guilty.

The South Carolina law pertaining to defense of habitation applied in Cyndi's case as well. Defense of habitation comes into play when a trespasser attempts to enter your home

1) in a violent manner or

2) with the intent to commit a felony on you or your home or

3) in an attempt to forcibly enter your home.

If even one of these conditions is satisfied, you are permitted to use deadly force against the trespasser, and you don't have to retreat before taking the life of the intruder.

These laws make it perfectly clear that in the State of South Carolina you have the right to expect safety inside your home. But the law doesn't stop there. It says you can use deadly force to protect yourself inside your home and that you don't have to retreat even if you can do so safely. The law doesn't stop there, either. It says you can defend yourself inside your home "without fear of prosecution or civil action." Obviously, the law is designed to protect people from criminals and from overzealous prosecutors. That is an important fact.

****

Now we need to examine the eyewitness statements. Below are critical excerpts from the affidavits taken by Druanne White and her staff from people who had firsthand knowledge about the shooting. These people gave statements to sheriff's detectives as well.

Garland Major who is Lieutenant of Investigations for the Anderson County Sheriff's Office gave me copies of the affidavits the detectives took on September 8, 2006. The main difference between the statements taken by the detectives and the ones taken by Druanne and her staff is the amount of detail they contain. Most of the statements taken by the detectives are very brief, and in critical areas, they are vague and imprecise.

Druanne and her staff did a better job of getting the eyewitnesses to open up and elaborate on the details. The points they drew out helped me to visualize what happened on the day of the shooting. I wasn't able to do that very easily when I read most of the statements taken by the detectives with two notable exceptions. The statement Mike Jackson gave to Detective McBride on the day of the shooting is clear and precise. In a moment, you'll see that Mike's statement was inaccurate, inconsistent, and contradictory, but that wasn't the detective's fault. I think Detective Vaughn also did a good job when he took Cyndi's statement even though Cyndi was in no condition at that time to give him a complete and comprehensive account of the incident and her Miranda rights were violated.

To be fair, Druanne and her staff did their work on September 9, 2006—the day after the shooting. That's important because the incident was still fresh in the witnesses' minds, and there was much less hubbub at the scene that day so they were able to take their time and talk with the witnesses in a more relaxed manner. That said, if the detectives were operating under a time constraint on September 8, 2006, it was self-imposed. Since this was a possible murder case, there was absolutely no reason to rush the investigation.

I relied primarily on the statements taken by Druanne and her staff for two reasons. First, as I said, I think they are better. Second, several eyewitnesses gave testimony in court under oath, and their testimony was consistent with the statements they gave Druanne and her staff in every significant detail.

****

The eyewitness testimony is telling:

- Billy Merriweather—a neighbor: "....I saw the little girl (Cyndi) on the porch. I saw the big girl (Amber) in the yard. I heard arguing and fussing. I couldn't tell what they were saying. Cindy (sic) went in the house. The door was shut. Amber was standing in the yard. Amber went up the steps and opened the door and went inside. The storm door shut behind her. I heard a loud pop and I saw Amber drop down. She was lying in between the door and the porch. Amber's boyfriend came to the scene. He said, 'call the police'....Amber's boyfriend yelled that Amber was shot in the head. Cindy (sic) was saying she didn't mean to shoot her. The law came. Amber's boyfriend had already pulled Amber out of the house. She was half way in the door. Her foot was still inside the door...."

- Vera Patterson—a neighbor: "....I have lived here for thirty-four years. Cindy (sic) and Justin have been my neighbor (sic) for about two years. They were good neighbors. They worked everyday. (sic) There was no violence or loud noise at their home. Cindy has never been in any trouble, never caused any trouble. She was a hard worker....I was inside the house when the shooting happened. My grandson was here. We were inside the house talking. I heard one bang. My grandson said, 'that was a gun.' It took me a few minutes to get to the front door. My grandson grabbed the phone and came out. The boyfriend was yelling 'call 911.' I'm not sure when the boyfriend got there. He was standing over Amber when I got to my front door."

- Trad Gunter—Vera Patterson's grandson: "...As I was coming down Roosevelt Dr. I saw a heavy set white female crossing Shawnee Dr. and she stopped in the middle of the road as I was turning in. I had to stop for her. She appeared to be high on something....The female went to 312 Roosevelt and stood at the front door. The boy (Mike) and girl (Amber) were conversing back and forth. I could not tell what they were saying. I then went into house. (sic) As soon as I sat down I heard a gunshot. I jumped up grabbed the phone and ran outside. (sic) I saw the girl that I saw (walking in the street) on the porch at 312 Roosevelt laying on her back with her left leg up under her. The white male (Mike) that I saw earlier go to 314 Roosevelt was kneeling over her trying to do CPR...."

- Sonya Mattress—a neighbor: "....Billy (Merriweather) and I walked outside. I heard loud shouting. I began walking toward Cynthia's house. Amber came across the street with flip flops in her hand. Cynthia came out of the house and said get out of my yard and went back in the house. Amber came up on the front porch. She jerked the door open. This was the storm door. The wooden door was open.

Amber stepped inside the house. Amber was yelling. She was angry. I then heard a shot. I couldn't see Cindy. (sic) She was inside her house. Amber had stormed inside. She fell back when she was shot. I ran up closer to the scene. Amber's boyfriend had been in his house. He ran out of his house and over to Cynthia's house and pulled Amber out of Cindy's (sic) house. He began performing CPR. I saw Cynthia on the phone coming to the door. The boyfriend asked me to help him and I asked if it was safe to come up. I came up to the door. Amber was not responding. Amber's boyfriend said, 'you shot her in the head'. Cynthia said, 'No, I didn't mean to.' Cynthia was scared and crying. She kept walking back and forth...."

- Tom Isom—a neighbor: "....I wave at Ms. Marchbanks and I have spoken to her one time. She always waves and her husband is the same way. I do not know Amber. I would see Amber going to the Marchbanks' house and I would see Ms. Marchbanks take Amber and her boyfriend places.

  On the day of the shooting I was in my garden. I heard a shot. I did not know where the shot came from. I saw Amber's boyfriend dragging Amber out of Cynthia's house. I saw the boyfriend give Amber CPR. I heard him say, 'Call 911.' I did not want to get involved. I went back to my garden. I did not hear any arguments before the shot. One policeman asked if I saw it. I told him I as (sic) in my garden and heard a shot. A detective came and asked if anyone had talked to me. I told him I had already talked to one of the patrolman. (sic)

  I think a lot of Ms. Marchbanks and I hope she gets out of jail and comes home to her dog. She has never caused any problems in the neighborhood. She and Justin have always been quiet neighbors who minded their own business."

- Betty Beebe—a neighbor: "....Cynthia and Justin were friendly neighbors. Cynthia offered to help me if I needed anything. She is a very sweet and considerate person. I never saw any violence from Cynthia and Justin's house. Cynthia did not interfere with people. As soon as Cynthia would get home from work, Amber would go over to Cynthia's to get a ride. Cynthia barely had time to get out of the car before Amber would be there. I even saw Amber carrying laundry over to Cynthia's for Cynthia to do her laundry. Also, Amber did not have any water and she would go over to Cynthia's with two buckets to get water daily. On September 8, 2006, I passed Amber and her boyfriend walking down 81 on my way to White Jones. This was around 9:30 a.m."

- Edward F. Beebe, a neighbor—husband of Betty Beebe: "I know Cynthia. She and Justin are our neighbors. They are quiet. They stay at home. I never heard any noise or seen (sic) any violence from their house. They have been our neighbors for one year or so. Cynthia and Justin have offered to help my wife and me with our chores. They wave to us everytime (sic) they leave the house.

Justin and Cynthia worked all the time. Amber lived beside Cynthia. Amber always came over to Cynthia's when Cynthia got home from work. It appeared Cindy (sic) and Justin were being used. They gave Amber and her boyfriend rides. Cindy and Justin worked hard and right when they came home it appeared that Cindy had to give them a ride every day to work. Cindy (sic) and Justin never complained. It looked like they had to wait on Amber and her boyfriend all the time. On the Tuesday before the shooting, Amber dragged over her dirty clothes to Cynthia's house. My wife said, 'Look, they are making Cindy (sic) do their laundry.' Amber would carry water to her house from Cindy's (sic) house daily. Amber would do this in the morning and in the evening. I could clearly see.

On September 8, 2006, I had picked up the paper and was drinking coffee. I was sitting on my front porch. My wife had gone to White

Jones. While I sat there, I could see a couple coming down the street, walking from 81 toward Cynthia's house. I paid no attention. They went by my house. I looked up. I later realized the couple was Amber and her boyfriend. They got to the center of the intersection in front of Cynthia's house. The man walked to his and Amber's house. The woman headed for Cynthia's house. Both of Cindy's (sic) doors were closed. The woman came and really banged hard on the door. I heard it from my house. It was very hard banging. Cindy (sic) did not come to the door. Amber started to walk back to her house. Cindy (sic) opened the door. Cindy (sic) had a towel in her hair. Amber came back to Cindy's (sic) door. Amber yelled at Cindy (sic). There was a lot of cussing but I could not understand everything that Amber was yelling. Amber was yelling but Cindy (sic) was not. I heard Amber say, 'You have a gun, do you?' Cindy (sic) was in the house. I walked back into my house to get the phone and walked back to the door. As I was doing this, I heard a loud pop. I looked out and saw Amber's head go down. I called 911...."

****

As you know, Mike Jackson wasn't an eyewitness to the shooting, but he was directly involved in the incident, and he had pertinent information to share. Below are critical excerpts from the two statements he gave to Sheriff's Office detectives:

- From Mike Jackson's first statement given to Detective McBride on September 8, 2006 within minutes of the shooting: "Cindy (sic) got mad about her car's window tint being scratched. Cindy (sic) was pissed off and said who is going to pay for my tint. We told Cindy (sic) we would send her some money from Maryland. Cindy was pissed and left us at the pawn shop....Amber and I walked home from the pawn shop. (sic) The walk took us about fifteen minutes....I have never heard or seen any kind of violence between them (Amber and Cyndi)."

- From Mike Jackson's second statement given October 19, 2006 to Detective Matheson: "We made it to the red light just outside of the pawn shop (sic) and Cindy (sic) said to get the fuck out of her car....I asked her why she shot her and she said that she was coming in the house. She didn't seem upset or anything, it was as if she had thrown a rock at her instead of a bullet...."

There are unmistakable discrepancies between Mike Jackson's two statements, and interestingly, neither one of them is accurate. Mike told Detective McBride on the day of the shooting that Cyndi drove off and left him and Amber at the pawnshop. That is unforgettable. I think it's something he certainly would have remembered within minutes of it having happened, especially since it's a vital part of the story he told the detective. Mike also told Detective McBride that it took him and Amber about 15 minutes to walk home. I think that part of his story is correct.

More than a month later, Mike told Detective Matheson that Cyndi drove him and Amber to the first stoplight before she ordered them to get out of her car. That, too, is unforgettable and very different from the account he gave in his first statement. Problem is EZ Pawn is 1.8 miles from Cyndi's house, and the stoplight nearest the pawnshop is 1.7 miles from Cyndi's house. It is not physically possible for an overweight, pregnant woman to walk almost two miles on a hot, humid day in 15 minutes.

In the statement that Cyndi gave to Detective Vaughn, she said that she drove Amber and Mike to the intersection of highways 81 and 28 before they got out of the car. That's one mile from EZ Pawn and 8/10 of a mile from her house...or about a 15 minute walk. I know that because I've been there; I measured the distances; and I walked the route.

A thorough examination of the facts reveals that Cyndi's version of the events on September 8, 2006 is correct. As she said, she had nothing to hide, and she was trying to be cooperative. It is also apparent that the detectives did not look into the details of Mike Jackson's account. In particular, they didn't attempt to verify his story by measuring the distances prior to 11:30 a.m. on September 8, 2006 when Detective Matheson charged Cyndi with murder. I think it's fair to say that on the day of the shooting Detective Matheson did not realize he had serious problems with the testimony of his star witness. However, on October 19, 2006, those problems should have been patently obvious.

****

There is other evidence that corroborates the eyewitness testimony that Amber was actually inside Cyndi's home. The information below is taken from a South Carolina Law Enforcement Division (SLED) Forensic Services Laboratory Report dated October 4, 2007 by Edward A. Porter, Forensic Scientist:

- At the request of Assistant Solicitor Catherine Huey…to determine if the victim (Amber Robey) was actually shot outside on the porch or inside the residence of 312 W. Roosevelt Drive, Anderson, SC.

- After examination of all evidence available, the following conclusion can be rendered: the victim, identified as Amber Robey, was standing at or in the threshold of the door of 312 W. Roosevelt Drive when she was shot.

- From the SLED report commenting on witness statements:

    ➤ Frank Beebe: "He heard Amber screaming at the suspect and beating on her door….the victim tried to entice the suspect in the yard to fight."

    ➤ Anderson County Coroner's Office: "Paramedics found decedent lying supine on front porch of residence with feet inside front door."

> Deputy Holbrooks' supplemental report: "While exiting the residence with the handgun and Cynthia, I did observe a spent shell casing lying just inside the door beside the front leg of the couch."

> "Dr. Brett Woodard (the pathologist who performed Amber's autopsy) stated that the victim (Amber Robey) suffered a brain shot with the bullet severing the victim's spinal cord. Dr. Woodard stated that this trauma would have immediately incapacitated the victim, making the victim unable to move her arms or legs. Dr. Woodard stated further more (sic) that the victim fell down immediately, with gravity, once she was shot, and did not make any further movements."

After examining the evidence including eyewitness statements, the state's forensic expert concluded that Amber was shot at or inside the threshold of Cyndi's home. The eyewitness testimony is so clear that you need help to be confused. Cyndi's neighbors said that Amber broke into Cyndi's house and that she was shot inside Cyndi's house. The prosecutor had every bit of this information before the trial.

****

Below is the text of a letter from Druanne White to Catherine Huey dated October 10, 2007:

Dear Catherine:

My investigator has attempted to contact and interview law enforcement witnesses about the referenced case. As you know, my client is facing very serious charges that hold very serious consequences. To our surprise, the law enforcement witnesses informed my investigator that they were instructed not to talk to the defense. When I discussed this with you yesterday, you informed me that you had talked to Captain Tommy

Williams about this issue. Apparently Captain Williams has forbidden his officers from talking to the defense. You told me yesterday that you had talked to Captain Williams and that you had instructed him that it was his choice, but it would be better if the choice was "inform".

I was a prosecutor for almost twenty years. I am shocked that law enforcement would not talk to both the prosecutor and the defense. I always thought that the State had a duty to present the truth in an unbiased manner. I am happy to have the officers record any interviews with my staff, or for their Captain (or anyone else) to witness the interviews. Apparently I will need to make a motion on this issue. I will probably also need a continuance in order to properly prepare this case for trial.

On another note, you mentioned for the first time yesterday that the State has performed blood spatter tests in this case. (The italics are mine.) Please fax me the results so that I may decide whether or not the defense needs a continuance to get its own expert.

Thank you for your assistance in this matter.

Sincerely,
Druanne White

This letter indicates that Catherine Huey notified Druanne White about the state's blood spatter evidence on October 9, 2007. That's less than two weeks before the trial. I called the Solicitor's Office three times to find out when they received the forensic expert's findings from SLED, but they were uncooperative. Hence, I obtained a copy of the report and discovered that the letter conveying it from SLED to Catherine Huey was dated October 4, 2007.

Druanne's letter raises another important issue. Forbidding prosecution witnesses from talking with the defense is unlawful. That tactic was used by another prosecutor in South Carolina and the defendant received a life sentence.

The jury verdict was reversed on appeal (The STATE, Respondent, v. Brad Edward WILLIAMS, Appellant, No. 24609, Supreme Court of South Carolina.) because according to the Supreme Court of South Carolina "…the state unconstitutionally intimidated a potential defense witness, causing the witness to refuse to be interviewed by the appellant's counsel. We find appellant has established prejudicial error on this ground, and reverse and remand." Obviously, despite what Catherine Huey told Captain Williams, the decision to allow prosecution witnesses to talk with the defense was not his to make.

****

Examining the evidence means more than simply taking statements. As I've pointed out already, most of the detectives who took statements from Cyndi's neighbors didn't draw out the same level of detail that Druanne and her staff did. That means Detective Matheson did not have the kind of comprehensive information he needed to make an informed decision. As an experienced detective, he should have known that.

Additionally, we don't know what Detective Matheson told the solicitor, and we don't know what she told him. However, since he charged Cyndi with murder following that conversation, we know for certain that he/they believed they had enough evidence to support murder charges. You've seen the evidence. What do you think?

But there were other problems with this investigation. The statement Mike Jackson gave on the day of the shooting was internally inconsistent and contradictory. Unfortunately for Cyndi, that fact was never discovered because the detectives didn't examine his statement carefully. But this is a murder investigation, so we have the right to expect in-depth work on the part of the professionals at the scene. If the most important witness, the only substantive witness, tells a story that is inconsistent or if it makes no sense, then law enforcement authorities have no business using his testimony to charge anyone with a crime, much less murder.

79

This is the bottom line. The detectives did not take the time to conduct a thorough investigation. I'm not speculating here. That's what the evidence shows very clearly. If law enforcement authorities had performed their jobs properly, they would have obtained more complete information from Cyndi's neighbors. Had they done that, without a doubt they would have had serious questions about Mike Jackson's statement. In all likelihood, the uncertainty would have created reservations in their minds and would have caused them to delay filing murder charges against Cyndi until they could complete a more in-depth investigation.

This is the inescapable truth. Even a perfunctory examination of the other evidence at that point would have convinced them that Cyndi acted in self-defense. Still, there was an opportunity to correct that grievous error. Detective Matheson took a second statement from Mike Jackson about 6 weeks after the shooting. I think it is obvious that he did not compare the two statements for consistency and accuracy. The lack of consistency is self-evident. As for accuracy, simply measuring distances as I did reveals that neither of Mike's statements is believable. Therefore, he was an unreliable witness and that fact should have been evident on September 8, 2006. It was reinforced when he gave his second statement.

Those problems did not prevent the solicitor from accepting Mike Jackson's statements without reservation or qualification. I'm not speculating here either. The theory of the case presented during Cyndi's trail was based on Mike's allegation that Cyndi shot Amber because of the torn window tinting. On top of that, the solicitor rejected Cyndi's self-defense claim and the testimony of Cyndi's neighbors who actually witnessed the incident. Most important of all, though, the solicitor completely ignored South Carolina's laws regarding self-defense and defense of habitation because the evidence shows clearly that Amber broke into Cyndi's house to do her serious bodily harm.

But there's even more you need to know. The solicitor had other relevant information about Mike Jackson long before Cyndi's trial. For instance, at only 26 years of age, he had managed to build an impressive criminal record. His offenses were many and varied. Common sense would suggest that his background should have been taken into consideration by the solicitor. I believe she should have seen Mike's past and the discrepancies between his two statements as serious problems, but obviously she didn't. Why? For your information, Cyndi had no criminal record. Her slate was completely clean.

Finally, SLED's Forensic Services Laboratory Report corroborated Cyndi's claim of self-defense. Nothing in it even hints at murder. It's no wonder Catherine Huey didn't introduce the SLED report as evidence or call SLED's forensic scientist to the witness stand.

****

At this point, you know what the law says about self-defense and defense of habitation. You've also seen the critical portions of the affidavits from the people who saw the shooting, heard the gunshot, and/or had firsthand knowledge of any type to share about the incident. All of this information was, or could have been, available to the prosecutor within days of the shooting.

If you give any credence whatsoever to the solicitor's case, you must believe that Cyndi Marchbanks mapped out a plan to kill Amber Robey in the 15 minutes it took for Mike and Amber to walk from the intersection of highways 81 and 28 to Cyndi's house. But that's not all Cyndi did during the 15 minute interval in question. She drove home, took Amber's purse to her house and put it on the front porch, looked for the phone, called Justin, took a shower, and dried off. That's a lot of activity for a 15 minute period. Obviously, there wasn't very much time for "planning."

But we shouldn't stop there. To buy the solicitor's argument, you have to believe that Cyndi Marchbanks, a young woman who had never had any problems with the police, shot Amber Robey because of a tiny scratch on her car's window tinting that would have cost at most a few dollars to repair. Until that very moment, she had been the best friend to Mike and Amber that anyone can imagine. As far as I'm concerned, that stretches believability beyond any reasonable limit.

****

While I was a full-time professor at the University of Virginia, I did consulting work for the Federal Bureau of Investigation (FBI) and the Drug Enforcement Administration (DEA). Because of my involvement with them, I had to have more than a layman's knowledge of law enforcement. That's why this case puzzles me. It's obvious to me that Cyndi acted in self-defense. The law is unambiguous, so I believe the charges against her should never have been filed.

I talked with several of my associates who are in law enforcement about this case—some at the federal level and some at the local level. Every one of them agreed with my conclusion that 2 hours of investigation was far from adequate, especially since the charges were so serious.

There was absolutely no reason to rush things. They could have waited for weeks or months or even years to file charges. So why hurry? Why did Detective Matheson and the solicitor push ahead with murder charges against Cyndi so quickly when there was no credible evidence that she even broke the law? In fact, there was abundant evidence that she acted in self-defense.

One of the law enforcement professionals I spoke with said that the detectives must have been in a hurry to finish so they could go to lunch. He was kidding, of course, but that explanation makes as much sense to me as any other. Based on what I know, I find it very difficult to believe that a team of law enforcement professionals from Anderson County South Carolina looked at the same evidence I saw and concluded that their investigation was complete in less than 2 hours.

Think about what Cyndi and her family had to endure. For almost 14 months, they lived with the constant fear that Cyndi would have to spend the rest of her life behind bars. The prosecutor had to know how much pain and suffering the Marchbanks family was experiencing because of her decision to pursue murder charges against Cyndi. You've seen the evidence and the law. Do you think the solicitor had a case?

Druanne White summed up Cyndi's predicament on September 8, 2006 succinctly:

"It's obvious that Cyndi acted in self-defense. Picture this. You're inside your home. You're alone. Someone comes into your home to hurt you. You point a gun at them and tell them to leave, but they keep on coming until the end of the gun barrel is 6 to 12 inches away from their face. At that point, you have to use the gun, or that person will disarm you and use it."

Druanne's explanation makes perfect sense to me.

****

Druanne White served as solicitor before Chrissy Adams. I asked her if it was unethical for the solicitor to move ahead with murder charges against Cyndi given the complete lack of evidence supporting those charges. This is her response:

"When I was the solicitor, I looked in the mirror and said, 'You will never, ever make a decision based on politics.' But I was a one-term solicitor. I'm not accusing anyone of anything. I'm just telling you what I think. This case should never have been tried....Several people told me that if I had been the prosecutor, I would have won the case. I said, 'No. If I had been the prosecutor, I never would have tried the case because for me it would not have been ethical.'

As a prosecutor, you have an ethical duty to the truth. This was a high-profile case. It was hard to dismiss. I had to make some tough decisions when I was in that job, and some of them weren't popular. I don't care how you explain it. It's still not going to be popular. That's why as a prosecutor you have to say, 'I'm going to do what's right even if it costs me my job.'

I wasn't penalized for doing the right thing. In fact, God rewarded me handsomely. When I opened my practice, it took off immediately. My husband and I have been foster parents for many years, so I have birth and non-birth children. Since I'm no longer a "government worker," they can work with me. Nepotism rules would have prevented that from happening in the solicitor's office. Because my income increased substantially when I opened my practice, I can afford to send all of them to college. Right now, 2 of them are in college, and one is in law school. If I had been reelected, paying their tuition would have been very difficult without taking on a mountain debt. God really does look out for us."

I've included the American Bar Association's Rules of Professional Conduct for prosecutors as Appendix 2. Take a look at it and decide for yourself if the solicitor adhered to minimal ethical standards for prosecutors.

Chapter 8
The Trial

There's no reason to present a blow-by-blow description of the trial because you've already seen the evidence and the law. In this chapter, I'll focus on a few things that demonstrate how weak the prosecution's case was. It will help to explain why the jurors were able to complete their task in less than 2 hours.

****

Judge Buddy Nicholson was on the bench for Cyndi's first bond hearing and her trial. "Judge Nicholson treated me and my family well from the beginning—like I was innocent until proven guilty," Cyndi said.

"Druanne told me to plan on spending the week of my trial in jail. That's the normal procedure, but Judge Nicholson didn't make me stay in jail that week. He said, 'You're going to come back, right?' I smiled and said, 'Yes sir, your honor.'"

"Druanne told me that the assistant solicitor, Catherine Huey, could have asked the judge to lock me up during the trial, but she agreed to let me stay out of jail. She also agreed to let me leave the state to visit my family even though my bond prohibited me from leaving South Carolina. I really appreciated that."

Cyndi's trial lasted 4 days, including one full day for jury selection. "During jury selection," Cyndi said, "the potential jurors were asked if they had heard about my case. Most of them had heard about it, and most of them said that based on what they knew, they thought I was guilty. All of them said that they could reach a guilty or a not guilty verdict, depending on the evidence."

"During the week of the trial, I spent the evenings with my family and stayed with Justin at night. Druanne told me that she felt good about our case, but she also said, 'You can't predict what a jury will do.' In case we lost, I wanted to spend as much time as I could with the people I love. If we lost, I would be in prison for the rest of my life."

****

Cyndi was sitting in our living room as she told me about the week of her trial. After she left that evening, I tried to put myself in the frame of mind she must have been in that week. Candidly, it was impossible to do because I couldn't make myself believe I might be spending the rest of my life behind bars. I suspect you have to experience that situation to fully appreciate what Cyndi was going through.

Even so, I did try to imagine the fear she must have felt, the dreadful thought of being locked up day after day after day after day... endlessly until the day I died. It reminded me of a time when I was a small boy. I think I was 4 or maybe 5 years old. My mother was telling me about heaven, and she was explaining eternity in that context. Of course, I wanted to know something about hell too, so I asked her, "Do people who go to hell have to spend eternity there?" She said, "Yes, they do."

That's the day I decided that I didn't want to go to hell. You may think I'm trying to be funny, but I'm not. Tying together those two things—hell and eternity—made me realize that I didn't want to take any chances. I wanted to go to heaven. I think the week of Cyndi's trial was her "heaven or hell" week. That was when she really understood for the first time what she would be giving up if the jury found her guilty. While Cyndi explained what happened, I couldn't help thinking about how unfairly she had been treated by law enforcement officials in Anderson County.

****

If you've taken the time to sit through a jury trial, you know how tedious they can be...for the people in the audience. If, on the other hand, you're the defendant in a jury trial, things are anything but boring. It's amazing how focused you can be when you may be experiencing your last few days as a free person. You concentrate on all the little details, no matter how insignificant they are.

"Amber's parents came to court each day dressed very neatly," Cyndi said, "...like they might be heading to church or to a fancy restaurant. It surprised me because I had never seen them dressed up before. Amber's father cut off his ponytail for the trial. He shaved, too, and he was wearing kaki pants and a Polo shirt. They didn't even look like the people I knew. In fact, they looked like an all-American family. Before the trial, I don't think Amber's father even owned a pair of blue jeans without holes in them. Mike dressed up for the trial too. He has tattoos up to his neck. He wore clothes that covered most of them. I couldn't help looking at all of them and wondering what the jury must be thinking."

"During the trial, I tried my best to pay attention. It wasn't easy, though. So much was at stake. Most of the time, I kept thinking about how my life could change in a matter of days. This thought kept running through my mind, over and over and over: *At the end of this week, my life as a free person may come to an end.* I was as nervous as I've ever been, so nervous that I threw up...more than once." Cyndi started laughing as she recalled getting sick to her stomach in court. "During the trial, I tried to make as much eye contact with the witnesses and the jury as I could. I really did try hard to pay attention, but it was difficult."

It was obvious to me that Cyndi paid closer attention to the goings-on at her trial than she realized. She laid out the details in perfect order. While she explained what happened, I could imagine her giving her statement to Detective Vaughn on the day of the shooting. Even though she was nervous, she did an outstanding job. Her courage and strength under extreme pressure enabled her to stand firm when weaker people would have collapsed. Cyndi may have been nervous during the week of her trial, but she was as alert as she could be.

Neil Snyder

****

A jury trial is as much stage show as anything else. It has drama, suspense, and action—some of it manufactured especially for the jury. It's like a Broadway play being performed for 12 ordinary people who will ultimately determine the fate of the defendant. The jurors are a lot like you and me. They enjoy a good show. It engages and entertains them. Courtroom drama isn't mysterious to good lawyers. They are notorious for using theatrics to play on the emotions of jurors. After all, they know that juror's feelings can be as decisive as the facts in a close situation.

Cyndi's case was tailor-made for a solicitor who was seeking re-election. Chrissy Adams had good reason to believe that her lack of experience in the courtroom and her tendency to plea bargain tough cases would become issues during the campaign. Cyndi's case gave her a perfect opportunity to show the people of Anderson, South Carolina that she was tough on crime and that she didn't coddle criminals.

Cyndi could feel and actually see the drama unfolding before the trial even began. "I knew it was going to be an uphill battle. The press had already portrayed me as a scoundrel and as a cold-blooded killer. On top of that, Catherine Huey, the assistant solicitor who tried my case, was pregnant during the trial."

Cyndi shook her head and laughed. "It looked to me like she was almost 9 months pregnant, and she wore tight clothes. I mean really tight clothes. When the trial was over, one of the jurors told me that the only day Mrs. Huey didn't wear tight clothes to court she was so thankful because she thought the baby could finally breathe. I guess she wore those clothes to show off her belly and try to win sympathy for Amber from the jury. There may have been other lawyers in the Solicitor's Office who could have tried my case. I don't know, but having a pregnant woman do it seemed suspicious to me."

"The first time I saw Mrs. Huey was before the trial. She was going from door-to-door in my neighborhood talking with my neighbors. I thought, *I'm doomed*. This isn't fair. Mrs. Huey is very pretty. You know how much sympathy people feel for pregnant women. I don't blame them. I do too, so I thought, *It's all over for me. I'm going to spend the rest of my life in prison.* It was interesting, though. I could tell that the jury tried not to look at her. When Druanne got up to question a witness, it was different. All of them paid close attention to everything she said."

If the solicitor assigned Cyndi's case to Catherine Huey because she was pregnant, her strategy failed. The jury probably felt the same way I did when I examined the evidence. The thing that stood out in my mind was the injustice done to Cyndi and her family. That said, assigning Cyndi's case to an attractive, pregnant prosecutor may have been many things, but I can't help but believe that it was not coincidence.

****

The prosecution needs to tell the jury a story that makes sense to obtain a guilty verdict…most of the time. It's called their theory of the case. All the facts of the case should line up behind it in a reasonable way, or the jury will probably reject it under most circumstances. Catherine Huey told the jury in no uncertain terms that Cyndi Marchbanks was a cold-blooded killer, so she had to show them facts to back it up. Problem is she didn't have any facts to support her theory.

"I think the prosecution made a big mistake," Druanne White said on a Saturday afternoon in her office. "From the very beginning, they tried to cast Cyndi as a villain. They said she was a horrible girl who killed someone because of scratched window tint…that she was a cold-blooded murderer. There was nothing in Cyndi's background supporting that claim…nothing at all."

Cyndi doesn't look like a killer. She's young and attractive; she's jovial; she's friendly; and she's witty. But looks can be deceiving. To successfully portray Cyndi as an arch villain, the prosecutor needed to show the jury something in her background that pointed in that direction. Problem is Druanne was right. Cyndi's background contains nothing suggesting that she is even mean-spirited; much less that she is a cold-blooded killer.

"That was Catherine Huey's theory of the case. It really surprised me. It was ridiculous given Cyndi's past. Nobody is going to believe that someone who works full-time, has never had any kind of criminal record, and has never had any violent encounters with anybody is suddenly going to murder her best friend over scratched window tint. That doesn't make any sense at all."

"Trying to portray Cyndi as a cold-blooded killer was really over the top," Druanne continued. "If they had said that she killed with malice and forethought, that would have satisfied the requirement for murder, but that's not what they said. They said that Cyndi thought it all through and planned the killing the way a real cold-blooded killer would do. The jury didn't buy it."

As you know, only one individual who saw the incident or had anything to do with it gave testimony that was critical of Cyndi in any way. That person was Mike Jackson. The prosecution's case depended on him and his version of the events on September 8, 2006. If he failed to convince the jury that Cyndi was guilty, then the prosecution's case was destined to fail.

****

"Mike Jackson was the prosecution's first witness," Druanne said. "Catherine asked him if he had ever been in trouble before. That was a mistake, a serious mistake, because it opened the door for me to walk through. When witnesses take the stand, there are significant limitations on what you can do to impeach their testimony. I couldn't ask Mike if he had ever been in trouble before. But once Catherine asked that question, since I knew there were things out there that I couldn't normally get in under the rules of evidence, I could bring them up because she opened the door. I was able to get into evidence all of Mike's prior arrests for a wide range of serious offenses."

When I finished writing an early draft of this chapter, I asked Druanne to read it since I quoted her a great deal. In that draft, after Druanne explained why she was able to introduce Mike Jackson's criminal history into the record, I said opening that door was a demonstration of the prosecution's incompetence.

Druanne objected to that conclusion. She told me that sometimes good lawyers make mistakes in the heated give-and-take of a trial and that Catherine Huey is a competent attorney. I'll defer to Druanne's judgment about the prosecutor's competence, but this much is certain. As a result of that prosecutorial error, Druanne was able to show the jury a side of Mike Jackson that the prosecution didn't want them to see. His credibility in their eyes was damaged and possibly destroyed by his own words. For Cyndi, it was a blessing in disguise.

"Mike inadvertently did a lot to help our case by telling the jury that Amber and Cyndi were best friends," Druanne said, "that she drove them all over town, that she helped Amber get a job, that she tried to help Mike get a job, and that Amber and Cyndi had no problems until that day. That wasn't consistent with their theory of the case. The jury thinks with its heart, not with its head. Mike was their star witness, and his testimony didn't fit at all with the cold-blooded killer theory."

"Mike said that he didn't like living in Anderson," Druanne continued. "That didn't help him with the jury. You don't want to tell people who are from Anderson that you don't like their town. When Cyndi took the stand, she said she loves Anderson, and she really meant it. She moved back here because she loves Anderson, and she still lives here despite all the adverse publicity she has gotten because of the murder charges."

"The prosecution argued that Amber went over to Cyndi's house to get her purse, and for no other reason, but Mike told the jury that he yelled over to Amber as she was walking to Cyndi's house that her purse was on the porch. In fact, he said that he showed Amber the purse. That ripped a big hole in the middle of their case because obviously she was heading to Cyndi's house for another reason. It wasn't about her purse at all. There was absolutely no reason for Amber to go over there except to raise cane."

****

Cyndi had an interesting perspective on Mike Jackson's testimony. "He lied about everything. He testified that Amber said things she didn't say, and he testified that I said things I didn't say. For example, he said that he was in the bathroom of their house when he heard Amber say, 'Gun, gun, gun. What are you doing with a gun?' That didn't happen. How in the world could he have heard something like that if he was in the bathroom of his house and Amber and I were in the living room of my house? He was just lying."

"Mike said that he ran over to my house after he heard the shot and that Amber's whole body was on the porch...that she was never inside my house. Blood spatter witnesses for us and for the prosecution said that wasn't true. So did Mr. Merriweather."

"He testified that I said Amber deserved to die. For what? For scratching my window tint? That's ridiculous. I never said such a thing. I never even thought such a thing. He was just lying."

"When Mike came over to my house, he said, 'You shot her in the head on purpose.' I said I didn't do it on purpose and that's the only thing I said to Mike besides, 'Here's a towel. Stop the bleeding.' I was afraid of him. I didn't know what he was going to do."

"Druanne made it clear to the jury that Mike is a liar. She asked him if he had ever beaten Amber up, and he said, 'No.' Amber had filed an order of protection against Mike while they lived in Maryland, and he was not supposed to come anywhere near her because he beat her up so badly. Druanne had the police report, but Mike denied everything. He said that it didn't happen."

"After Mike denied it several times, Druanne pulled out the police report, showed it to him, and said, 'This police report says it happened.' Mike said, 'I was never convicted so it didn't happen.' After the trial was over, one of the jurors told me that his denial that day showed the jury what a liar Mike is. She said she couldn't believe he would deny that something happened just because he wasn't convicted of a crime."

"Mike yelled at Druanne while he was on the witness stand. He was really mad. The judge had to say something to him about it. His violent temper was on display in the courtroom for everyone to see, and the fact that he's a liar was clear too. Amber was just as violent as he is. When they got together, the sparks flew. I still think he was her biggest problem."

It should interest you to know that the woman from EZ Pawn who bought the television set from Mike and Amber told me that she was on the prosecution's witness list. She also said that she was prepared to testify, but she was never called. Why? I can only guess, but the fact that Mike Jackson destroyed the prosecution's case may have had something to do with it. Ms. Huey may have realized after his testimony that the case was lost.

****

Instead of helping the prosecution's case, Mike Jackson's testimony probably doomed their efforts from the very beginning. Even more, his testimony proves beyond any shadow of a doubt that there was no evidence that Cyndi committed the crime with which she was being charged.

Cyndi's neighbors punched holes in the middle of the prosecution's case as well. They explained what happened so clearly that the jurors could see that Cyndi acted in self-defense.

"Billy Merriweather did a lot of damage to their case," Druanne explained. "He said he saw the big girl yelling...that's Amber. He said he saw the little girl, Cyndi, motioning with her hands for the big girl to go away. The hand gestures he used on the witness stand indicated that Cyndi was telling Amber to 'get out of my yard.' He said the little girl went inside her house, and the big girl went up on the porch and started jerking the door. He said he saw the victim being pulled out of the house by Mike Jackson before he did CPR."

"Mr. Meriwether saw everything," Cyndi said. "He testified that he heard arguing. He said that Amber was screaming at me, and I said, 'Just go home.' He saw Amber come up on my porch and jerk my storm door three times. He told the jury that he heard the pop as she tore the door open. He saw her come into my house and the door close behind her. Then he heard the shot and saw Amber fall straight down and backwards so that her head was on my doormat. That's exactly what happened."

"Frank Beebe, one of my neighbors, also testified," Cyndi said. "He told the jury what a nice neighbor I was and how quiet we were. He said we never caused any problems. Then he talked about Mike and Amber coming to town. He said they were always over at our house, and he talked about them carrying water from our house to their house. That must have amused my neighbors. Mr. Beebe testified that he went inside his house to call the police before the gunshot. When he came outside, he saw Amber most of the way on the porch. Mike had already pulled Amber out by the time he came outside."

****

The physical evidence and the prosecution's theory of the case were just as weak as Mike Jackson's testimony. From top to bottom, the case against Cyndi Marchbanks was totally without merit.

"Catherine said that Amber was on the porch, that she never entered Cyndi's house," Druanne said. "There was a circular pool of blood on the doormat with a void of blood in middle of the pool. The doormat was on the porch right in front of the door. Catherine said that's where Amber's knees were, but there were no blood stains on the knees of Amber's jeans."

We were in Druanne's office when she showed me that it was impossible for the void of blood on the doormat to be caused by Amber's knees. She reenacted the event for me to prove beyond any shadow of a doubt that the shooting couldn't have happened the way the Catherine Huey said it happened.

"There would have been blood on Amber's jeans if her knees had been on that mat," Druanne said. "The spot in the middle of the doormat that was void of blood is where Amber's head was, and the blood pooled around her head. Mike pulled Amber out of the house when he came over. That's what the evidence showed. This is a critical point because it proves that she was in the house."

"Also, Amber had no bruising on her head or her knees. If she had fallen on the porch there would have been bruising because it's cement and very hard. The absence of bruising indicated that she fell on the carpet inside the house. The prosecution didn't have any evidence that would stand up."

****

Catherine Huey didn't even call her own forensic expert to the stand...for obvious reasons. His testimony would have driven a stake through the heart of her case. Druanne had to hire one herself, at Cyndi's parents' expense, and she called him to the stand. In so doing, Druanne was able to introduce the state's forensic evidence by asking her witness if he agreed with the findings of SLED's forensic expert. He testified that he did agree with the state's expert. In the end, both of them concluded that Amber was inside Cyndi's house when the shooting occurred.

"They didn't introduce their own blood spatter expert's testimony because it contradicted their theory of the case," Druanne said. "It's as simple as that."

Cyndi was somber as she told me about the SLED forensic expert. "I think it was a big deal to the jury that the prosecutor had a blood spatter expert that she didn't call because his testimony proved my case. And the expert they did

95

call gave testimony that had nothing to do with his expertise. One juror said that any one of them could have given their opinion, and that's all his testimony was...his unqualified opinion. Druanne told me that the law says they have to tell the defense about exculpatory evidence, but they are not required to call their own witnesses. Based on what their blood spatter expert said, they should have dismissed the charges against me. There never should have been a trial."

****

Cyndi was the final witness. She spent 90 minutes on the witness stand. "After I finished telling Druanne exactly what happened, Catherine Huey said, 'Well, you've added a lot to your testimony now that you've heard what your neighbors had to say.' She was referring to the statement I gave Detective Vaughn. I told her that I was in shock that day. There's no way I could have told him everything, and besides, he wrote what I told him in his words. I thought the police would want to talk with me again, but none of them talked to me after that day."

"Mrs. Huey made me read my statement to the jury, everything except the part about Amber's drug use. She asked me why I didn't say this and why I didn't say that. I just repeated what I said before. 'I was in shock. There's no way I could have given a perfect account of the incident that day.' Even so, what I told Detective Vaughn that day was pretty close, and the discrepancies she focused on were minor."

"No defendant gives every single detail in a written statement," Druanne said. "I ask the jury to think about it. If something happened to them and they wrote a letter about it, they would put many details in the letter, but not all of them. If they were explaining what happened to a friend, they would have a lot more to say."

****

"One thing in particular happened during the trial that proved to me that God really does exist," Cyndi said. "Mike Jackson had a new girlfriend by the time the trial started. She came to court with him. On the day he testified, the jury was coming back from lunch, and they saw Mike sitting on the courthouse steps making out with her. He wasn't just kissing her, either. He was kissing her passionately…the way you don't kiss in public. If he had any credibility with the jury before that incident, it must have evaporated. That's what one juror told me after the trial was over."

Making out with his new girlfriend on the courthouse steps probably did as much to undermine Mike Jackson's credibility in the eyes of the jury as anything else he did or said on the witness stand. According to Cyndi, "Being spotted by the jurors as they returned from lunch is exactly the kind of thing that God causes to happen. God has subtle ways of getting His points across. I feel the same way about the prosecutor's 'mistake' that allowed Druanne to introduce Mike's criminal record. Under normal conditions, good prosecutors don't make those kinds of errors."

Chapter 9

The Jury Reaches a Verdict

Jury trials aren't science. Juries are swayed as much by emotion as facts, and they have been known to do some outrageous things over the years. For instance, there's the classic case of the elderly woman who sued McDonalds and won several million dollars because she spilled a cup of hot coffee in her lap. The jury determined that McDonalds had a duty to warn the woman that the coffee was hot. That's the nature of a jury trial, and both the prosecution and the defense know it. In some ways, it's like rolling the dice or tossing a coin.

In some ways, jury trials are like the game of baseball. They have a saying in baseball. It's not a ball or a strike until the umpire calls it. Courts of law are similar in this respect. Until the jury reaches a verdict, you're neither guilty nor not guilty. You're simply the defendant. But there is one thing a jury can't say, and it's something Cyndi desperately wanted to hear: "You're innocent."

Innocent and not guilty are very different. The government attempted to convict Al Capone numerous times but failed because it didn't have enough credible evidence and live witnesses. He was the head of organized crime in Chicago in the 1920s, and he was as guilty as sin, but he walked out of court time after time as a free man. No one thought of him as innocent. Eventually, he was convicted of income tax evasion and sent to prison. The wheels of justice turn slowly, and at long last, Al Capone was found guilty and got what he deserved.

Innocent means the prosecutors were wrong from the get go because you didn't commit a crime. You should never have been dragged into court in the first place. If you're innocent, that's what you want the jury to say. You want to be able to walk down the street or into a restaurant and have people look at you and know that you're innocent. If you're simply not guilty, they may look at you and think that you got off on a technicality the way a common criminal would. You're guilty, but....

****

The amount of time that lapsed between the conclusion of the trial and the reading of the verdict was less than two hours. It was a torturous 2 hours for the Marchbanks family and for Druanne White. All of them knew that Cyndi was innocent. She didn't commit a crime. Amber Robey was the culprit. She broke into Cyndi's house to beat her to a pulp, or worse, but there was still a chance that Cyndi would have to spend the rest of her life in prison.

"I was really scared on the last day of the trial," Cyndi said. "I kept thinking, *This is the end of my life. There's not enough time.*" Reliving the last day of her trial was obviously an emotional experience for Cyndi. Her voice was cracking as she stopped for a moment to wipe a tear from her eye. "I thought, *This may be the last time I ever see my family outside of prison.* I couldn't stop thinking about it. Everything was happening so fast. I was the last witness, and I was on the witness stand for an hour and a half. When I got off the stand, they had closing arguments, and then the judge dismissed the jury so they could deliberate. I wanted to leave the courthouse because I was so nervous. My heart was beating about 100 miles an hour, and I was sweating a lot."

"There were 3 alternate jurors. They couldn't deliberate with the 12 regular jurors. They came out and said 'their verdict' would have been not guilty, but they didn't know what the regular jurors would do. They were ticked off because they wanted to vote. Druanne told me that was a positive sign, but they were just alternates. The only people who mattered at that point were the 12 jurors in the Jury Room."

"I knew the alternates didn't have a say in the matter, and I didn't want anyone to give me false hope. I couldn't take that. I didn't want to be let down at that point. I had already been humiliated in front of my family, my friends, everyone who knew me, and people who went to school with me. I didn't want anyone to tell me they thought the verdict would be 'not guilty' unless that's what the jury said."

"After we had waited for an hour, I told Druanne that I had to get out of there because I was feeling sick again. If this was going to be my last few hours as a free person, I wanted to spend my time with my family...not in front of all the people in the courthouse."

"We drove to my house, and we were there for a few minutes before the jury came back in. While we were at my house we got calls from people all over the place. There were so many people praying for me. People I didn't even know were praying for me. I really appreciated that. When we got to my house, we turned on the television. They were playing my testimony on the news."

"That was an eerie feeling. I started crying. It tore me up watching that person on TV talk about what happened. I felt so bad for her having to relive that terrible moment, and then I thought, *That's me*. It hurt me to see myself telling about watching Amber's body fall. I couldn't stop crying. That was the first time I felt sorry for myself...the first time I didn't want to be Cyndi Marchbanks. I can still see myself on the witness stand pleading with the jury to believe me. My life was in their hands, and I desperately wanted them to know that I was telling the truth."

"When we got the call to come back to the courthouse, I was so scared that I could hardly breathe. It's a short ride to the courthouse. They rushed us into the courtroom. We sat there and waited. It didn't take that long, but it felt like an eternity. I kept thinking, *O God, this is it. O God, this is it.* I was shaking involuntarily when they brought the jurors in. One-by-one they filed in and took their seats. One woman on the jury smiled at Druanne. She leaned over and whispered in my ear, 'I think you're going to be okay.' I didn't want to hear that. I wanted to hear the jury say it."

****

Falsely Accused

"The judge came out, and the jury foreman gave him the verdict. When they read the verdict on the first charge I just fell to the floor. I can still hear it, 'NOT GUILTY.' I said, 'Thank you God.' I was so thankful. I could hear Druanne. She said the same thing. 'Thank you God.' We were all praying."

"The jury could have found me guilty of murder, guilty of manslaughter, or not guilty. Once they decided that I was not guilty on the first charge, all of the other charges disappeared."

At long last Cyndi was free...truly free. But just as important from her point of view, 12 people, a jury of her peers, had examined all of the evidence and determined that she was not guilty, that she had acted in self-defense. She was not a murderer. In fact, she was innocent. If only the jury could have said that. Even so, fourteen arduous months of paralyzing fear for Cyndi and her family had come to an end.

****

"They took Amber's family out of the courtroom first. I was still excited about the verdict, but I cried as I watched them leave. I felt so sorry for them. I thought, *I didn't want to hurt Amber. I didn't go over to her house, break in, and threaten her. I tried to avoid trouble. I put her purse on her porch. She didn't have any reason to come over to my house.*"

"Sam Frazier, the deputy who called me a murderer on the day of my bond hearing and threatened to tase me, walked me and my family out of the courtroom to our car. On the way out, we stopped for a few minutes and talked with the jury and media people. When Deputy Frazier walked me over to the van, he said, 'From the first time I read your file, I knew that it was self-defense. We just want to tell you that if anything ever happens and you need help, just call us.' I appreciated that, but why did he call me a murderer, and why did he threaten to tase me on the day of my bond hearing?"

****

It took the jury less than 2 hours to reach a verdict. The date was October 25, 2007. That's the other big day in Cyndi's life. "Not Guilty." Cyndi said. "God gave me another chance. I'm so thankful. My life could have been over that day, but it wasn't."

"Every prosecution witness supported my case...every single one of them except Mike Jackson. And I guess you can say that he supported me too because he revealed himself to the jury and destroyed his own credibility. Even their blood spatter expert supported my case. They didn't call him to the witness stand, but I think his absence was more powerful in the minds of jurors than his presence would have been."

"I wouldn't wish on anyone what the prosecution put me through. I'm glad Druanne White was my attorney because she's smart, and she's a worker. She kept me from going to jail for defending myself. This is what I really have a hard time believing," Cyndi said as she stared straight into my eyes. "The people responsible for prosecuting criminals and protecting the public were using my case for something completely different. I told you that I was naïve, but this is the real naiveté. Deep down, I wanted to trust them, but in their eyes, I was trophy game. They wanted to take my head and mount it on their wall. The fact that I was innocent was irrelevant to them."

****

Cyndi Marchbanks will have to accept the fact that some people she knows will wonder about her. After all, she was accused of committing murder—a double homicide. That's all some people know, and it's all they care about. The accusation itself is good enough to sway their thinking. The question of guilt or innocence isn't terribly important to them, and there isn't a thing she can do about it.

Very few people in the Anderson community who have heard about the shooting actually know the facts. Most of the people that I've talked with personally have only a vague recollection of the incident, but they do remember these grisly details. A pregnant woman was shot in the face; her unborn daughter was delivered postmortem; and the baby eventually died. Oh, and by the way, the shooter was a girl named Cyndi Marchbanks. Cyndi will have to live with that stigma for the rest of her life. Thankfully, she won't be living in a prison cell.

Chapter 10
The Family Suffered Too
and For What Reason?

This is a parent's worst nightmare. All of us have thought about it…probably several times. The phone rings. You wake from a sound sleep. The voice on the other end of the line says, "Mrs. Jones, your daughter has been in an accident."

Immediately, you break out in a cold sweat. Your heart skips a beat. Fear takes hold of you. "Is she alright," you ask frantically.

There's a pause. It seems like an eternity. You're afraid of what the answer might be, but you want to hear it just the same. "She's in the hospital….," the voice says. You breathe a sigh of relief before you know the extent of her injuries. Maybe she has broken bones or scars on her face; she may be missing a limb; she could be in a coma; but thank God she's alive. You wouldn't wish that phone call on anyone.

The effects of this call can be just as devastating. "Mr. Marchbanks, your daughter is in jail. She's being charged with murder." Make no mistake, the decision to charge Cyndi Marchbanks with murder imposed a horrendous penalty on the entire Marchbanks family.

****

Bobby Marchbanks, Cyndi's father, took the call. It was a little after noon, and Gwen, Cyndi's mother, was at lunch with some friends from work. Bobby called Gwen on her cell phone and asked if she was alone. She told him she wasn't, so he asked her to excuse herself and leave at once. Only after she was away from the group would Bobby tell her what happened. That day, their lives and the lives of every other member of the Marchbanks family changed forever.

"When I first met Amber," Gwen said, "I didn't want Cyndi to be friends with her, but when you're middle school age, you have to start making your own decisions. Besides, at that age, the more you push kids one way, the more they want to go the other."

"Cyndi was very popular in school in South Carolina. She didn't know what to make of the fact that the kids in her class in Maryland didn't want to be friends with her. In that situation, you take the first friend you can get, and Amber was Cyndi's first friend."

"I could tell from Amber's attitude that she wasn't the kind of person I wanted my daughter to be around, but I didn't want Cyndi to be without friends either. I told Cyndi how I felt, but I didn't tell her that she couldn't spend any time with Amber."

Gwen started crying. "I blame myself for so much. I could have told Cyndi she couldn't see Amber, but I didn't. When Cyndi told me that Amber was moving to South Carolina, I had a terrible feeling about it. I could have said something then too. I was thinking, *This is not a good idea.* I had no clue what was about to happen, but with Amber being the kind of person she was, I didn't think any good could come from it. I knew Amber was a bully, but I really didn't know how dangerous she was."

Bobby joined in. "Cyndi didn't tell us a lot of things until we got down here."

"I knew that Amber and her boyfriend had had a lot of problems," Gwen said. "Like I said, I blame myself. I should have said more. I should have told Cyndi, 'Don't do that.' I blame myself for not doing more in middle school. I should have been stronger with my opinions."

****

While Gwen was talking, Katie and I looked at each other. Both of us had tears in our eyes. I think it would have been difficult, maybe impossible, for any parent to sit there and not be touched emotionally by Gwen's and Bobby's discussion about how they felt.

Gwen blamed herself for what happened. She thought she could have done something to prevent it. But that's not realistic. Bad things actually do happen to good people, and there's nothing you or anyone else can do about it. Still, parents, mothers in particular, want to believe they can move mountains where their kids are concerned. They think they can prevent bad things from happening to their children. It's a dream...make-believe, but they think it nonetheless.

****

"Because of my job," Bobby said, "we took Cyndi away from all of her friends in Anderson. We felt guilty about that. We took her to a new environment where she had no friends. Everything was new. I don't remember too much about Amber from those days, but I do remember this. It was the day Gwen picked up Cyndi from Amber's house. That evening she said, 'Bobby, you wouldn't believe Amber's father. He looks like he belongs to a motorcycle gang. I'm not comfortable with Cyndi spending time over there.' I remember that vividly, but that's about the only thing I remember."

"The media in Anderson said that Cyndi and Amber were best friends," Gwen said, "but that wasn't true. They had been best friends in middle school for one year, but they hadn't been best friends since then. In high school, they were acquaintances. After high school, they talked on the phone, and that's all. Amber played on her friendship with Cyndi in middle school when she asked for Cyndi's help, and Cyndi's the kind of person who would do just about anything for a friend."

Gwen looked at Bobby and said, "You don't remember Amber very well because she didn't come to our house very much, and I wouldn't let Cyndi spend time at their house. Amber didn't like the fact that I wouldn't let her smoke at our house. She told Cyndi, 'If my parents don't have a problem with it, I don't think your parents should have a problem with it either.' Almost all of their interaction was at school even when they were 'best friends.'"

****

"Amber didn't have any true friends," Gwen said. "If she had other friends, I don't think she would have reached all the way back to her middle school years and called Cyndi. I think she had burned all her bridges, exhausted all her friendships, and she wasn't getting real friendship, the kind of friendship that tries to help you, from members of her own family. Cyndi was the only friend she had left...the only person who would listen to her. The other people who knew Amber were through with her, but Cyndi still listened. Cyndi didn't call Amber 3 times a week. Amber called Cyndi until Amber decided she was moving to South Carolina."

"Amber knew good and well that Cyndi would help her," Bobby said.

"Amber's family started a website," Gwen said. "I haven't seen it, but my other daughters have. One thing that was said on the website was that Cyndi went out into the yard, put a gun to Amber's head, and pulled the trigger. The things people have said about Cyndi in the media are totally off base...not even close to the truth, but if you don't know any better you might believe what they're saying."

It was obvious that Gwen could still feel the emotional pain from their 14-month ordeal. "One little girl Cyndi went to school with said, 'That doesn't sound like the Cyndi Marchbanks I knew. She used to go out of her way to help a mentally challenged kid who was in school with us. Unless she's really changed, they're not talking about the Cyndi I knew.'"

107

Neil Snyder

"When they chose the jury for Cyndi's trial," Gwen said, "every one of them said they thought Cyndi was guilty based on what they had read in the newspaper or seen on television. After the trial, one of the jurors went by Cyndi's house and left a note on her door. Cyndi called her, and she said, 'We knew you were innocent. I just want you to know that.' Another juror told my sister-in-law to tell our family that she wanted us to know that God was with us in that Jury Room."

"From the beginning, we told everybody we knew to pray for us, but we didn't know until it was over just how much prayer support we had. Whole churches that we had nothing to do with were involved. When I got back to Maryland after the trial, I was told about one prayer group that went from Ohio down through Kentucky. People we didn't even know were praying for us. One woman came by Cyndi's house after the trial and told Cyndi that her preacher had their whole church praying for her because he didn't think she was guilty. Another woman told Cyndi's grandmother that they had 6 churches praying for her."

"My aunt, Levine Whitworth, was a real prayer warrior. She spent 3 or 4 hours a day praying. She was in a wheelchair, and she didn't go to the trial. She rarely even went out of her house, but the last day of the trial, the day Cyndi testified, she felt God leading her to go to the courthouse. She came to the bond hearing too, because she put up her property for Cyndi's bond. She said that God led her to come to the trial on the last day so she got ready because she knew someone was going to call and volunteer to take her. In a little while, sure enough, she got the call."

****

"I think Levine being there gave Cyndi the courage and strength she needed to testify," Gwen said. "None of us, Cyndi included, knew what to expect. All of us were worn out, and when Levine showed up in her wheelchair it made a world of difference. God had been answering our prayers all along. Three people volunteered to put up their land for Cyndi's bond. When Hailey died, there was another bond hearing, and we didn't know what to do. We don't own land in South Carolina so I got a home equity line of credit in Maryland to cover the second bond, but the judge let the first bond cover both charges. We were all praising God for that."

"It was so hard on us sitting in the courtroom. There were times when I was hurting so badly that I wanted to run out, but I couldn't leave my daughter in there all alone. I would say, 'God, it's in your hands. Just give us the strength to deal with whatever happens.'"

"I cried every day for almost 14 months. One day I was at work out on the patio transferring merchandise from one store to another, and out of the blue I just started crying. Someone sent the store manager out there to check on me. I told him that I was okay. 'It just happens,' I said. 'Sometimes it hits me, and I just start crying.' There were some praying people in that store too."

"Yeah," Bobby said, "one of the guys who used to work for me has his own church now. He's a minister, and he prayed with us on the phone. Anyone who doesn't believe in the power of prayer needs to talk with us for about an hour. I know for a fact that God honors prayer."

****

"I think about Amber's family, too," Gwen said. "I felt so sorry for them. If my daughter had been killed, I would want someone to pay, but they knew what a dangerous person she was. I think deep down they had a lot of guilt because of what they did and didn't do. I think they felt responsible."

"We grieved for Amber's family. Losing a daughter hurts. We know that because we almost lost a daughter. She could have been in prison for the rest of her life. We prayed for Amber's family every day. We especially prayed for Hailey until she died. She was completely innocent. That was a difficult loss for

Amber's family to take. We know that. I wanted them to know I was sorry for their loss, but I didn't dare say anything to them in court. It just didn't seem like the right thing to do. I thought it might make them angry and upset them even more."

****

"When I heard that you were going to write this book," Gwen said, "I didn't want it. I was against it. I said, 'I don't think that's a very good idea.' I just wanted to let it all die down. Now I think some good will come from it. Right now I think Cyndi is at a standstill in her life. She doesn't have a job...no benefits. She's searching, looking for direction. I think this might help her."

"Cyndi's a strong girl," Bobby said. "Once she finds the right direction, she'll say, 'It's time to move on.' You know, they say the true measure of a man is if he can bounce back when he hits rock bottom. Cyndi's going to bounce back."

"We went to Myrtle Beach for a week during the summer before the trial," Gwen said. "I wanted a family portrait, and I didn't know if we would ever be together as a family again. That may have been our last chance. We needed to spend that time together, even if it was just for a few days, and I wanted that picture so we went to the beach. There was a pier on the beach, and in the evenings they would play karaoke on the pier. Cyndi and her sisters sang together. They sounded so good, like angels. All of a sudden, I just started crying. I was thinking, *I don't know if they'll ever be able to sing together again.*"

"I read a newspaper article after the trial. It said the jury must have been influenced by a few tears. What a cruel thing to say. I saw the evidence. I guess the person who wrote that article didn't see it. But that was right anyway, and it wasn't a few tears. It was lots and lots of tears every single day for more than fourteen months, and lots of prayer too."

"You know what angers me," Bobby said. "As a family, we lost those 14 months of our lives over a case that they never should have tried. They didn't have any evidence, but they took 14 months of our lives that we can never get back."

"Cyndi called us 4 or 5 times a day from jail," Gwen said. "She was alone, locked up with criminals, and she wanted to talk with her family. I don't blame her. I felt the same way. They have a phone in the jail. It's through Paytel, and it's collect. It cost us $18 per phone call when Cyndi called. The total was about $90 a day for those calls while Cyndi was in jail, but I wasn't going to ask her not to call." Gwen started crying again.

"I don't care if it was $25 a call or $50 a call," Bobby said. "She was in a scary place, and she wanted to talk with her family. There's no way I was going to say, 'Don't call us.' She was surrounded by people who were not her friends, people who didn't have her best interests in mind. Cyndi needed to hear a friendly voice."

****

"The day Cyndi was testifying, Levine was sitting beside me," Bobby said. "Gwen was in shambles on my right. I'm supposed to be the strong father, but inside I'm ripped apart. I could hear Levine on my left whispering while Cyndi was testifying. I thought she was trying to get my attention, so I looked over at her. She was looking straight at Cyndi...staring at her and praying. I think that's the only thing that helped Cyndi get through her testimony. Levine wasn't crying. She wasn't upset. She just kept looking at Cyndi and praying. She kept saying one word over and over: 'strength, strength, strength.' She just kept saying that word."

Cyndi called Levine "Nana." Her coming to court that day meant a lot to Cyndi. "Nana was 81 years old. She died about 2 months after the trial." Cyndi's voice started cracking up as tears welled up in her eyes. After she wiped the tears away, she looked at me and said, "I hope my trial didn't contribute to Nana's death. I miss her so much."

Truth is no one knows for sure if Cyndi's ordeal had anything to do with Levine Whitworth's death, but we do know this. Levine's prayers were answered, and Cyndi's arrest and trial were indefensible, especially in a court of law. All of the evidence points in that direction. Every smidgen of it, and it should have been clear to law enforcement authorities in Anderson County South Carolina long before Cyndi's trail.

Chapter 11

Was It Prosecution or Persecution?

September 8, 2006 through October 25, 2007 was pure hell for the entire Marchbanks family. Cyndi was charged with horrific crimes that she didn't commit. If she had been convicted, she would have to spend the rest of her life in prison with no chance for parole.

The long-drawn-out legal process and the gut wrenching fear were almost unbearable. It's impossible to put into words the emotional toll it took on the Marchbanks family. And on top of everything else, Cyndi's mother and father had to shell out more than $30,000 for attorney fees and other costs, and her extended family secured Cyndi's release on bond by putting up their land. Needless to say, newspaper headlines reading "Woman Acquitted" or "Woman Not Guilty" were inadequate compensation following the jury's verdict.

"It just doesn't seem fair," Cyndi said. "They put my whole family through the wringer, and for what? I was just defending myself...inside my home."

****

Cyndi is innocent, and she has the court papers to prove it. Still, some people in the Anderson community see her as a cold-blooded killer. She'll have to live with it. That's what the jury thought too...before the trial. After examining the evidence, they voted unanimously to acquit her in less than 2 hours. If a single juror had thought Cyndi was guilty, the outcome would have been completely different. A hung jury would have raised serious questions about her that she would have had a hard time answering.

And Cyndi's ordeal isn't over yet. It probably never will be. To this day, she hasn't been able to find the kind of job she wants. Part of the reason is that she has to answer 'yes' to this question on an employment application: Have you ever been arrested? Following that question, most applications say something like this: "If the answer is 'yes,' list the offense(s)."

Take a moment and imagine what it's like for the person reviewing the application when he reads this list of alleged offenses:

- Two counts of murder,
- Death or injury to a child inutero, and
- Two counts of using a deadly weapon in the commission of a violent crime.

Do you think he cares in the slightest whether Cyndi was guilty or not guilty? Hardly. There must be hundreds, possibly thousands, of applicants for every good job, especially now with the global economy in a funk. Why take any chances? He would much rather hire someone who doesn't have an arrest record.

A couple of decades ago, IBM had such a commanding lead in the computer industry that purchasing agents for businesses would routinely buy IBM machines even if they were more expensive and weren't as good as their competitors' products. Their logic made a lot of sense. It all boiled down to the brand name: IBM. If something went wrong, the purchasing agent could simply say, "Well, I bought IBM." That explanation was more than adequate most of the time. The typical executive 20 years ago didn't know very much about computers, and she assumed IBM's products were the best, even if they weren't.

In Cyndi's case, anyone thinking about hiring her would have to ask this question. "If something goes wrong, what would I say?" They would have to justify their decision to higher-ups—people who don't care about the circumstances and the legal fine points. Keep in mind that Cyndi was fired from her job at O'Charley's for not reporting to work or calling in...from jail. The people who made that decision were probably using the same logic. Again, why take any chances if you don't have to.

****

Clearly, Cyndi is still a victim of law enforcement officials who ignored the facts and pushed charges against her for reasons that had nothing to do with the pursuit of justice. I asked Cyndi to reflect on how this experience changed her life. Below are some of the thoughts she shared with me:

—"I still think about it a lot. I can't help it. Questions keep running through my mind. *What could I have done differently? What were my options?* I know I was just defending myself, but that doesn't stop me from wondering."

—"I used to be happy, outgoing, and carefree. I'm more reserved now. I tend to hold back. I'm more careful than I used to be."

—"Now I know who my real friends are. There's this guy that I used to be friends with. We went to elementary and middle school together in Anderson. When I got out of jail, he wouldn't even talk to me."

—"Today, I don't trust a lot of people, and I don't like being around a lot of people. Most things seem so minor to me now because I'm alive and free."

—"I'm embarrassed when I go out in public. I think people are staring at me. I feel like everybody thinks I'm an evil person."

—"My family has been beside me from the beginning. They mean more to me now than they ever did."

—"Two years ago, my prayers were for insignificant things. I prayed for a parking space or for a green light. I've always prayed...constantly, but all of a sudden my prayer life changed. I was saying, 'O God, please don't take my life. You know my heart. You know what happened. You were there.' The little insignificant things just disappeared. Different things are important to me now."

— "Despite all I went through, deep down I knew God was with me. From the beginning, I could sense Him telling me that I was going to be okay. It wasn't going to be easy, but I would be okay."

Cyndi didn't mention the fact that she babysits for a woman who used to work for Druanne White. One of the woman's friends told her that she would never let Cyndi get near her children. You would have to meet Cyndi and get to know her to appreciate how preposterous that comment was, but it's a good example of the kind of attitude Cyndi has had to put up with every single day since the shooting.

****

Earlier, I asked this question. Was Cyndi Marchbanks Nifonged? I've examined the evidence in this case, and candidly, I can't understand how anyone can conclude that Cyndi didn't act in self-defense as that term is defined in South Carolina law. Obviously, the jury felt the same way.

What did the solicitor see in the evidence that the jury and I couldn't see? What were her motives? I don't know the answer to those questions, but I do know this. The evidence tells me that Cyndi acted in self-defense. Logic leads me to conclude that Cyndi was Nifonged.

The solicitor needs to explain why she didn't drop the charges against Cyndi when her own lack of evidence demanded that she should. Catherine Huey, the assistant solicitor, needs to speak up as well. She needs to tell us if she was just following orders or if she believed Cyndi was guilty of committing murder. These people have a lot of explaining to do. If they conspired to destroy the life of an innocent human being for political gain or any other reason, they should be held accountable.

It's important to point out that the parents of the Duke lacrosse players were wealthy individuals who could afford to hire high-priced lawyers to stand up for their children against the likes of Mike Nifong. If he had pulled the same stunt on college students with less well-to-do parents, the outcome may have been different. Parents with fewer dollars in the bank may have been tempted to hire less expensive but potentially incompetent or inexperienced attorneys who would have advised their children to accept plea deals to avoid risking the possibility of going to jail for the rest of their lives. Thankfully, Cyndi's parents aren't poor, but they're not New York investment bankers either. They had to dip into their retirement nest egg to pay for their daughter's defense.

****

Today, many people know about prosecutorial misconduct because of the Mike Nifong case. But his is just one example of a national problem that deserves a great deal of attention.

The Center for Public Integrity in Washington, D.C. analyzed 11,452 cases in 2,341 jurisdictions across the United States in which charges of prosecutorial misconduct were reviewed by appellate court judges between 1970 and 2003. In at least 2,012 of those cases, prosecutorial misconduct (i.e., reversible error) did occur. That's more than 17 percent of the cases involving charges of prosecutorial misconduct. In addition, the Center found another 513 cases in which appellate court judges submitted opinions suggesting prosecutorial misconduct, but they were in the minority so the verdicts weren't reversed.[3] These statistics are alarming.

The Center found that in 28 cases involving 32 defendants prosecutorial misconduct resulted in the wrongful conviction of innocent people who were later exonerated. Their convictions stemmed from a wide range of serious

---

[3] http://projects.publicintegrity.org/pm/

charges including murder, rape, kidnapping, and assault. In addition, the convictions of guilty defendants were overturned as a result of prosecutorial misconduct. In those cases,[4] hardened criminals who couldn't be retried due to double jeopardy rules were simply released back into the community because of prosecutorial misconduct. These outcomes are shocking and potentially very dangerous.

As you know, twelve ordinary citizens who saw all the evidence made up their minds about Cyndi Marchbanks' innocence in less than 2 hours. That's not much time when you consider that only a fraction of that time was spent deliberating. If you subtract out the time they spent eating and socializing, you begin to appreciate how little time it actually took the jury to reach a not guilty verdict. The truth was clear to them. Why couldn't the solicitor see it? Unfortunately, when I called her (several times) to speak with her about Cyndi's case, she wouldn't talk with me and she never returned my calls.

It may be coincidence, but the solicitor's secretary asked me what slant my book would take the first time I called. I noticed an immediate change in her voice and her demeanor when I said, "I'm just following the facts. I'll go where they lead me." I suspect that's why the solicitor never returned my calls, but I may never know for sure.

****

Flagrant prosecutorial misconduct is one thing, but there are other problems that demand attention as well. For example, as you know, many times innocent people are advised by their attorneys to accept plea deals rather than risk the outcomes of trials which can go either way. In Cyndi's case, that prospect didn't come into play, but as you know, it could have.

It would be foolish to believe that prosecutors don't know they're sending innocent people to jail many times when they make those plea deals. They know the drill as well as anybody, and they know the kind of advice many if not most

---

[4] http://projects.publicintegrity.org/pm/default.aspx?act=main

defense attorney's give to their potential clients—especially the ones who don't have a lot of money.

Cyndi could easily have become another casualty of our justice system. I wonder how many innocent people are in prison today because lazy or incompetent attorneys told them that they should plead guilty to crimes they didn't commit to avoid the death penalty or life in prison. The Center for Public Integrity's study didn't look at that offense, so I can only guess at how prevalent it is. I suspect the number is quite large though, probably much larger than the number of reported prosecutorial misconduct cases.

****

Most of the time, prosecutorial misconduct costs corrupt prosecutors nothing. Mike Nifong's case is not normal. He's an example of a prosecutor who actually had to pay for his crimes, and his criminal behavior has led some people, including me, to suggest that people like him are persecutors instead of prosecutors.

I don't believe there's a better way to describe people like him. They persecute innocent human beings for personal and professional gain. They are beneath contempt. Prosecutors have enormous power in our legal system. If they abuse that power, they deserve stiff punishment. As far as I'm concerned, their wrongdoing is even more egregious than the crimes committed by the real felons they seek to incarcerate who have no formal power in the system.

****

The Center for Public Integrity gave several examples of prosecutorial misconduct:

- "making inappropriate or inflammatory comments in the presence of the jury;

- introducing or attempting to introduce inadmissible, inappropriate or inflammatory evidence;
- mischaracterizing the evidence or the facts of the case to the court or jury;
- committing violations pertaining to the selection of the jury;
- making improper closing arguments;
- mishandling of physical evidence (hiding, destroying or tampering with evidence, case files or court records);
- failing to disclose exculpatory evidence;
- threatening, badgering or tampering with witnesses;
- using false or misleading evidence;
- harassing, displaying bias toward, or having a vendetta against the defendant or defendant's counsel (including selective or vindictive prosecution, which includes instances of denial of a speedy trial); and
- improper behavior[5] during grand jury proceedings."

From my perspective, it's prosecutorial misconduct if the prosecutor refuses to call her own expert witness to the stand because his testimony substantiates the defendant's claim that she was acting in self-defense. Technically, the prosecutor is not withholding exculpatory evidence, as you know. However, she is making an attempt to prevent pertinent information from reaching the jury. As far as I'm concerned, that qualifies as misconduct.

I also think that not calling the detective who charged Cyndi with murder to the witness stand was a serious mistake, especially since the prosecution's case was so weak. He said that he had "overwhelming evidence" that Cyndi committed murder. I believe he should have been questioned on the witness stand under oath. He should have been required to present his evidence.

I'm not trying to disparage the prosecutor's role in our legal system, but I do want to emphasize the critical importance of electing honorable men and women to that position. There's no question that it's a challenging job. According to The Center for Public Integrity,

---

[5] http://projects.publicintegrity.org/pm/default.aspx?act=main

"The top person in the office has a difficult job that tends to become more difficult every decade. That is especially so in major metropolitan areas, where the top prosecutor must manage hundreds of lawyers and support staff with a budget that always seems inadequate, deal with horrific crimes almost every day, think about prevention as well as conviction, all the while balancing the obligation to serve justice with the unavoidable scrutiny of won-lost statistics that become a factor in re-election campaigns. The difficulty has grown in medium-sized and small jurisdictions as well."[6]

If prosecutorial misconduct is prevalent in the prosecutor's office, it should be rooted out. The cost of dealing with the problem is insignificant compared to the cost of not dealing with it…especially to the innocent victims of corrupt and/or incompetent prosecutors.

****

Vince Lombardi, the legendary coach of the Green Bay Packers and the Washington Redskins, is remembered as one of football's greatest winners. As a football coach, he's one of a kind…a legend. One thing he said strikes me as particularly relevant here. He said, "Winning isn't everything. It's the only thing."

In our adversarial judicial system, winning has become the primary goal of many prosecutors. It shouldn't be that way, but it is, and it would be foolish to ignore reality. The payoff for prosecutors with winning records can be huge:

"The prosecutor's career path is enhanced by being, and being known as a 'winner', which enables the prosecutor to get more visible cases, and to obtain higher position and compensation in the prosecutor's office. Also, the career path for the successful prosecutor, as we have seen from the past, can go right up to the White House or to the position as Attorney

---

[6] http://projects.publicintegrity.org/pm/default.aspx?act=sidebarsa&aid=28

General or as a federal judge at any of the 3 levels (District Court, Circuit Court of Appeals and the Supreme Court)....The loss of a criminal case once commenced through obtaining an indictment can cause a major reversal in a prosecutor's planned career, and with such pressure to succeed, what difference (the prosecutor argues to himself) does it make if the prosecutor cuts a few corners here and there. The defendant is probably guilty, of something, if not the crime for which he/she has been indicted."[7]

As I've said before, the lack of credible evidence against Cyndi Marchbanks raises serious questions about the solicitor's motives. Even more, the evidence for self-defense in Cyndi's case was overwhelming. That's why I believe it's important for the solicitor to be given the opportunity to explain her decision. The assistant solicitor, Catherine Huey, needs to answer a few questions as well. Justice and equity demand it.

****

John Grisham is best known as a fiction writer. He turned courtroom thrillers into a money-making machine with books and films like *A Time to Kill*, *The Firm*, *The Pelican Brief*, *The Chamber*, and *The Runaway Jury*, to name just a few.

In 2006, Grisham published his first piece of nonfiction. It was a New York Times bestseller titled *The Innocent Man*. It's a touching story about Ron Williamson, a man from Ada, Oklahoma who was accused of killing a young woman named Debbie Carter. He was hounded by local police and finally arrested, prosecuted by a man who should have known better, and convicted of first-degree murder. After serving 11 years in prison as a death row inmate, he was exonerated and released from jail.

The Innocent Man is certainly worth reading. It's a great example of injustice, incompetence, and abuse in our legal system. As I've shown, these aren't infrequent or insignificant problems, and they touch and destroy real

---

[7] http://www.lawmall.com/abuse/abwhy.html

people's lives. It's time for us to hold law enforcement officials accountable for abusing our justice system. In fact, it's long overdue. They should adhere to the same high standards that the rest of us are obliged to follow.

If there is room in prison for innocent people like Ron Williamson and the Duke University lacrosse players and Cyndi Marchbanks, then there should be plenty of room in prison for prosecutors who ignore evidence or manufacture evidence to put him there.

Chapter 12
Unanswered Questions Remain

For more than a year, Cyndi and her entire family had to endure the pain of not knowing whether she would have to spend the rest of her life in prison. That's how our justice system works. By and large, it's a good system. For it to work properly, though, law enforcement officials must do their dead level best to be fair and objective. They have to consider all the evidence carefully and draw reasonable conclusions based on the facts because real people's lives are at stake.

"My mother was really upset because the prosecution didn't call their blood spatter expert," Cyndi said. "She didn't say anything in the courtroom, but when we got to the car after court that day, she said, 'I can't believe they've had evidence proving that my daughter acted in self-defense, and they went ahead and tried her for murder anyway. They didn't even call their own witness. I can't believe it.'"

I agree with Gwen Marchbanks. I think the solicitor needs to explain why the state's forensic expert wasn't called to the stand. I have other questions too...questions that I believe the solicitor should be required to answer if not by people in the legal system then by the Anderson, South Carolina community. For instance,

- Why was there such a long delay in getting the blood spatter report from SLED? We know that the solicitor received it on October 4, 2007—about a year after the shooting. That's too much time when you consider that an innocent person's life was hanging in the balance. There should be a very good explanation for that delay. Maybe the Solicitor's Office wasn't negligent in this case. SLED may be overworked and very slow, but we need to know for sure what caused the delay to avoid another case of gross injustice.

- Among other things, SLED didn't test for the fine blood mist produced when people are shot at close range. They should have. That evidence would have provided one more bit of proof that Amber Robey was inside Cyndi's house when Cyndi shot her. Someone in law enforcement at the state level should look into it.

- Why didn't the assistant prosecutor call Detective Kevin Matheson to the witness stand? I've mentioned this before, but he's the person who charged Cyndi with murder. In a written report, he said the evidence against her was "overwhelming." It's only fair to give him the opportunity to explain his logic especially since the jury didn't agree with him after a full-blown trial where all the evidence was presented. At the very least, I think it's fair to say that what Detective Matheson calls "overwhelming evidence" wasn't convincing evidence.

- Can the solicitor explain why a jury of Cyndi's peers reached a "not guilty" verdict in so little time after seeing all the facts and hearing the arguments from both sides? If the prosecution had had a case against Cyndi, even a weak one, I don't think that would have happened. Someone would have held out and insisted on a guilty verdict.

- What should we make of the fact that the assistant solicitor who tried the case was pregnant? Was she the only person who could try the case? Was she the best person for the job? I think this is an important issue because it points to questions about integrity in the Solicitor's Office.

- Why didn't the prosecutor drop all the charges against Cyndi once she had compelling evidence that Cyndi acted in self-defense? I suppose it would have been humiliating, and in all likelihood politically damaging as well, to dismiss the charges against Cyndi a couple of weeks before the trial, but that's when the SLED report arrived. Even if the solicitor believed Cyndi was guilty of murder, at that point, the evidence for self-defense was so overwhelming and convincing that I think common sense should have led her to drop the charges.

- Finally, why was Cyndi Marchbanks charged with 3 capital crimes that carry sentences of life in prison with no chance for parole when only two people died? A quirk in South Carolina law may permit a nonsensical piling on of charges, but logic and justice demand a rational explanation for the solicitor's actions.

****

After the trial was over, Cyndi came home one day and found a card from a juror on her front door. The message printed on the front of card said, "Best of Luck to You." Inside the card, the printed message read, "There are so many people who believe in you—now go take on the world!" And there was a personal note inside the card as well. It said, "Justin, you are an awesome man for standing by her. Cyndi, you are a very strong woman. You have been through a very tough time, and I commend you for carrying yourself so well. I hope that you can put all this behind you and start a new life. You are in my prayers. If you ever need anything, let me know." It was signed "Amber Day, Juror."

Amber Day can't know how much her card meant to Cyndi. It wasn't just another card because it came from a person who saw and thought about all the evidence against her. It came from a woman who voted to exonerate Cyndi after seeing the prosecution's case. Literally, Amber Day was one of 12 people who had the ability to send Cyndi Marchbanks to prison for the rest of her life, and she took the time to pen a note saying in essence, "You're okay, and it's time to move on." That can't alleviate the pain and suffering Cyndi went through, but it touched her heart in a powerful way and contributed greatly to her healing.

****

126

"I've thought about writing a book," Cyndi said. "I think I'll call it *Guilty Until Proven Innocent*. That's exactly what happened to me. I had to prove my innocence. Even though the jury found me not guilty, when I go into a public place, I can't help thinking that people are staring at me. I may sound paranoid, but most of the people in Anderson, South Carolina who know anything about me, know only this. I'm the girl who killed the pregnant woman. A few people know that I was acquitted. Very few people know that I'm innocent."

I analyzed the evidence in this case. I studied the laws in South Carolina pertaining to self-defense and defense of habitation. I spent many hours talking with Cyndi and Druanne White about everything associated with the shooting and the law. I spoke with detectives Matheson and Vaughn and talked with the woman at EZ Pawn, and I tried to talk with the solicitor and the assistant solicitor…several times. Many times during my discussions with Cyndi, there were opportunities for her to lie to me to make herself look good, but she never did, not even once. She always told me the truth. That's why I was not surprised by the jury's verdict.

No newspaper article and no short clip on television can lay out all the relevant facts in a murder case for people to think about, but this book does. When I started this journey, I wondered where it might lead. Now I know the answer. Cyndi Marchbanks is correct. She's innocent. She did not commit murder. She acted in self-defense. The jury saw it. Why couldn't the solicitor see it?

Neil Snyder

Chapter 13
Manufacturing Marijuana

Several small marijuana plants were found in Cyndi's house on the day of the shooting so she was also charged with manufacturing marijuana. I purposely delayed presenting this information until now. I wasn't trying to be deceptive, and I wasn't playing games. If I had introduced this subject earlier, it might have biased you. I didn't want that to happen since it has nothing to do with the murder charges. Besides, I'm following a good precedent. Druanne White argued successfully that the marijuana charge should be separated from the murder charges. None of the information in this chapter was presented to the jury during Cyndi's trial for the same reason that I didn't talk about it earlier in the book.

Not surprisingly, the marijuana charge raises more questions about the quality of "justice" meted out in Cyndi's case. Once again, you be the judge. Was Cyndi given a fair shake by law enforcement authorities in Anderson, South Carolina? So you'll know, Detective Matheson had all of this information at his disposal before he decided to charge Cyndi with murder on September 8, 2006. Did it influence his decision? He told me it didn't, but you be the judge.

****

Anderson is located a few miles south of I-85 in the northeast corner of the state very close to the Georgia border. It's about 100 miles from Atlanta and 150 miles from Charlotte, North Carolina. Drug running (especially cocaine, marijuana, methamphetamine, and heroin) along the I-85 corridor between Atlanta and Charlotte is big business. According to a 2007 report, the Drug Enforcement Administration (DEA) concluded that "South Carolina is an end user, a staging area, and a transshipment state for all illegal drugs."

The sheriff of Anderson County at the time of Cyndi's arrest, David Crenshaw, referred to the I-85 corridor as "a major thoroughfare for drug traffic." As he explained it, "The dope goes north and the money goes south. Typically, the meth comes up from Mexico. Atlanta is a big drug hub and Charlotte is, too. We're right smack in the middle of all that traffic." The Anderson County Sheriff's Office made almost 2000 drug arrests between 2005 and 2008, and the I-85 corridor accounted for 132 of those arrests.

In 2008, the Anderson County Sheriff's Office won a national award for its drug enforcement activity. Speaking about his efforts to deal with the mounting drug problem in Upstate South Carolina, Sheriff Crenshaw said, "We've had some real active enforcement, and because of that, we're not in as bad of shape as we were. We could use another eight (narcotics officers) tomorrow. There's plenty for them to do....Our Aggressive Crime Enforcement unit has done a tremendous job of getting out there and making arrests. As long as there are people who are using it, there will be people who are selling it. Our job is to get it off the streets."

****

According to a recent report,[8] since 1990 roughly 20.5 million people in the United States have used marijuana each year. The same report said that between 1990 and 2005 the highest reported marijuana usage by people in the United States occurred in 2002 with 25 million people using the drug. The lowest reported usage took place in 1992 with only 17.4 million people reportedly using the illegal narcotic. Another report[9] concluded that more than 83 million Americans over the age of 12 have tried marijuana at least once in their lives. That's roughly 25 percent of our population.

Those statistics and others like them can be found in frequently referenced reports such as the National Survey on Drug Use and Health and its predecessor—the National Household Survey on Drug Abuse. But drug use

---

[8] http://www.drugscience.org/Archive/bcr4/2Usage.html
[9] http://parentingteens.about.com/od/marijuana/a/teensmarijuanadruguse.htm

statistics are notoriously inaccurate due to chronic underreporting owing to the fact that they rely almost exclusively on self-reporting. For obvious reasons, most people are reluctant to admit that they use illegal drugs even when their identities are supposedly protected.

One report suggested that marijuana usage statistics for the United States should be at least 50 percent higher than reliable studies indicate. Another report[10] said that the usage statistics may be double what we routinely hear. I went to undergraduate school at the University of Georgia from 1968 to 1972. My best guess is that at least 75 percent of the students with whom I went to college used marijuana at least once during their undergraduate days, and UGA is a very conservative school...or so they say.

This is my point. At best, the marijuana usage statistics we read about tell us the bare minimum number of people in the United States who have used marijuana. If we knew the real number, we would probably be shocked.

The following example is revealing because it involves a group of people that most of us consider to be trustworthy. They also tend to be strong believers in law and order, and they are definitely not left-leaning in their political philosophy.

While I was a professor at the University of Virginia, I did consulting work for the Department of Defense including the United States Army Foreign Science and Technology Center (FSTC) in Charlottesville, Virginia. To do my work with FSTC, I had to obtain a top secret security clearance. Anyone who has ever been cleared at the top secret level knows how exhaustive the process is. While I was getting my clearance, people from all over the country contacted me and told me that federal investigators had visited them personally and asked about me.

I won't bore you with the intricacies of the security clearance process because it's not relevant for this discussion, but this part of the process is

---

[10] http://www.drugscience.org/Archive/bcr4/2Usage.html

pertinent. The final step before you get a clearance is a personal interview, and the interviewer asks all kinds of pointed questions. They are intended to put you on the spot. They're the kinds of questions that most normal people would rather not answer. This is one question they always ask: Have you ever used illegal drugs? For reasons that may not be readily apparent to most people, your answer to that question could determine whether you get a security clearance.

At the end of my interview, I asked about the drug use question. My interviewer told me that they would never rely on my answer alone. By the time they talked with me personally, they had already met with all the references I gave them plus other people I knew who my references told them about. In essence, they identified my contact network and talked to many people with whom I had been associated over my entire life up to that time. I knew some of them well; others I knew only casually; and others knew me, but I didn't know them.

By the time I sat down for my interview, the Defense Department investigators knew almost everything there was to know about me. At that point, they simply wanted to know if I would tell them the truth. My interviewer said that people who can't answer difficult questions truthfully are easy targets for blackmailers, and they aren't good security risks.

Without blinking an eye he continued. "Almost everyone in the United States who was born after World War II has experimented with illegal drugs…especially marijuana," he said. "We know that for a fact. We just need to know that you won't be vulnerable because you're afraid of being found out." That's more consistent with my personal experience than anything I've read in drug usage reports.

Please don't think that I'm trying to minimize the seriousness of the drug problem we face in the United States, and I'm not excusing people who use illegal substances, even casually. I'm certainly not denigrating the importance of drug enforcement activity. My sole purpose is to put things in the proper perspective, and this is what you need to take hold of. Most of the people in the

United States today—including most politicians, judges, sheriffs, sheriff's deputies, detectives, solicitors, assistant solicitors, and other law enforcement officials—have experimented with marijuana. You have to ignore mountains of hard evidence to draw any other conclusion.

If you have any doubts, consider these facts. Bill Clinton, a two-term President of the United States, admitted that he smoked marijuana while he was in college, but he didn't inhale…or so he said. It was reported and is widely accepted as fact that George W. Bush, another two-term president, and President Barak Obama used cocaine at one point in their lives. Again, given what we know, it's foolish to believe that today's law enforcement officials don't have first-hand experience with illegal drugs, especially marijuana.

****

The nature of the investigation at Cyndi's house on September 8, 2006 took a dramatic twist when the detectives discovered a small container holding embryonic marijuana plants. But that day the detectives only thought they were marijuana plants.

I believe their heightened sense of awareness where illegal drugs are concerned might have caused the detectives to commit a serious fact-finding error. Instead of homing in on the shooting which was their primary objective, they may have focused their attention, or too much of it, on the suspected illegal drug. Suddenly, Cyndi wasn't just the suspect in an alleged murder case. She was possibly linked to narcotics trafficking. I believe that may help to explain why Detective Matheson charged Cyndi with murder before conducting a thorough investigation.

****

"Manufacturing marijuana." Those words have an ominous ring to them, but they simply mean growing marijuana. It has nothing to do with quantity. Unfortunately, that's not common knowledge.

The manufacturing marijuana charge added rocket fuel to the media feeding frenzy surrounding Cyndi's high-profile "murder" case. To appreciate the effect it had on the Anderson community, picture yourself sitting in your easy chair reading the newspaper or watching the evening news. The story is about a shooting incident that took the life of a pregnant woman, and the shooter was "manufacturing marijuana" in her home.

What thoughts run through your mind? To me, it sounds like Cyndi turned her house into a marijuana factory. There were probably rooms full of illegal plants growing to the ceiling. There was a big drug deal. It involved a large sum of money. Things went haywire. A scuffle ensued over possession of the valuable contraband. Shots were fired. One of the people involved in the fracas was a pregnant woman. A bullet pierced her body, and she was killed.

Actually, that didn't happen. I'm purposely being overly dramatic because I want to emphasize a point. Our imaginations can do amazing things. In the absence of accurate, detailed information, our minds fill in the gaps by conjuring up storylines that rival the plots in Hollywood blockbusters and New York Times bestsellers.

I think that happened here. Cyndi was made to look like a drug-dealing, gun-toting moll by media people who jumped all over the salacious aspects of the story. It's easy to understand why they did it. Sensationalism attracts viewers, listeners, and readers. At the end of the day, media people are playing a ratings game. The larger the audience, the more money they make. It's just that simple. Regrettably, they didn't follow through as professional journalists ought to do and report all the relevant facts of the case.

I'm not suggesting or implying malicious intent on the part of anyone in the media. I'm just talking about sloppy journalism, and it's not uncommon. We've grown accustomed to getting our news in fast paced, 30-second snippets. That's what we want, and journalists are more than happy to oblige. We're being fed a diet of half-truths and innuendos that are skillfully packaged and smoothly delivered by talking heads and glib writers. It's as much show business as journalism.

Because journalists didn't do their jobs properly, people reading or hearing about the shooting had to complete the story as best they could. Alas, most of them knew only these details:

- A pregnant woman was shot and killed.
- The shooter was manufacturing marijuana in her home.
- The victim's baby was delivered postmortem.
- The child died 40 days later.
- The shooter was charged with a second count of murder.

The conclusion should be obvious to most readers and television viewers. A drug deal went very badly. Cyndi Marchbanks is guilty of murdering two people. Case solved. It's time to move on to the next news item.

****

This is what actually happened on September 8, 2006. The container "discovered" by detectives at Cyndi's house was a flower pot in the kitchen that had been left out in plain view. In it were 20 miniscule marijuana seedlings. The detectives also found a book on the kitchen table explaining how to grow marijuana. It was impossible to miss because it was next to the pistol.

To put it in perspective, the flower pot was about 7 inches in diameter. That's smaller than a bowling ball. The total amount of marijuana in the flower pot wasn't enough to roll one tiny marijuana cigarette, or joint.

I've talked with a lot of people in the Anderson community about this case. Most of them jumped to conclusions that are consistent with the dramatic movie adaptation I presented, but it doesn't resemble what really happened. Point is Cyndi Marchbanks was unwittingly victimized by the press. It doesn't matter if it was intentional or unintentional. The result is the same.

Falsely Accused

****

At the time of the shooting, both Cyndi and Justin were casual users of marijuana. Neither one of them denied that fact, but the plants originally belonged to Justin—not Cyndi. He admitted it and turned himself in to the police. In case you don't know this already, marijuana seeds accompany the illegal drug when you buy it. Justin simply tossed a few seeds into the pot. He didn't even water them. He just put the pot on the porch in plain view and forgot about it.

According to Cyndi, when Mike and Amber came to town, Mike noticed the tiny seedlings and got excited. He thought he could grow the plants for sale. He already had a book on marijuana cultivation. That's the book the investigators found on the kitchen table. Mike took control of the plants, but he didn't take the flower pot to his house. Unfortunately for Cyndi and Justin, he left it at their house since he and Amber didn't have running water.

There is no question that Cyndi and Justin were culpable in this matter. Throwing seeds into the flower pot was foolish...especially since neither one of them had any knowledge about South Carolina's laws pertaining to manufacturing marijuana. I'm not alleging or implying that ignorance of the law is an excuse. I'm simply pointing out a fact.

Allowing Mike Jackson to leave the flower pot at their house was even more reckless. By law, the marijuana was Cyndi's and Justin's responsibility because the flower pot was inside their house. There is no denying that fact. What's more, according to South Carolina law, Cyndi was just as responsible as Justin even though she never had anything to do with the plants. That just goes to show how serious the consequences can be for things that young people think are not a big deal. Well, it was a big deal as both Cyndi and Justin would soon discover.

When the detectives found the plants, they obtained a search warrant and went through Cyndi's and Justin's house with a fine-toothed comb looking for anything suspicious...anything that might be drug related. The only thing they found was that small flower pot with 20 tiny seedlings, and as Cyndi said, they were actually Mike Jackson's plants.

****

Cyndi's murder trial ended in an acquittal on October 25, 2007. The drug charge was finally resolved on December 19, 2008. That's more than two years after the shooting and more than a year after Cyndi was acquitted by a jury.

The drug charge ended with a plea deal. Cyndi pleaded guilty to misdemeanor marijuana possession; she had to surrender her driver's license for 6 months; and she had to pay a $645 fine. She was allowed to obtain a restricted driver's license to drive to and from work.

The assistant solicitor, Catherine Huey, could have thrown the book at Cyndi. If she had done that, it's very likely that she would have obtained a conviction because the flower pot was inside Cyndi's home. The penalty for manufacturing marijuana is 15 years in prison. Cyndi would have been eligible for parole after serving 85 percent of that time, or 12.75 years.

Cyndi is very thankful that she was allowed to plead guilty to avoid a prison sentence, and she's glad her ordeal is finally over, but Justin was responsible for the plants. He admitted it. In addition, that was Cyndi's first offense of any type. It's customary for people to plead guilty on a first offense for a nonviolent crime and have the charge expunged from their record after 3 years if they don't commit another offense. Cyndi wasn't given that opportunity. The misdemeanor drug charge will remain on her permanent record.

****

Hippocrates, the ancient physician, said, "Healing is a matter of time, but it is sometimes also a matter of opportunity." He was right. Healing takes time. More than 2 years after the shooting, people Cyndi doesn't know still recognize her. One woman saw Cyndi in the local video store where she works, and she wrote a letter to Cyndi's manager telling him that he had no business employing such a notorious person.

Although Cyndi is innocent, she has to prove herself every day to people she doesn't even know, people who assume she's the monster they read about or saw on television. Memories fade. In due course, Cyndi will find the right opportunity and win over most of her skeptics...at least she will win over the ones who really matter, but Hippocrates was right just the same. It takes time.

Chapter 14

Not Guilty and Innocent
are Light-years Apart

Appendix 3 contains anonymous comments that were published in the online editions of local papers during the week of Cyndi's trial and selected comments about the case that are posted on the Internet website www.topix.net. I made no attempt to edit them.

You already know the facts surrounding the shooting and the relevant South Carolina laws pertaining to it. You know that the law explicitly says that you can protect yourself and others inside your home with deadly force if need be, and you can do it "without fear of prosecution or civil action." That's crystal clear. In addition, the law says that you do not have to retreat inside your home even if you can do so safely. That's unequivocal. You also know that 12 jurors most of whom believed Cyndi was guilty before the trial examined the evidence and declared that she was not guilty—that she was simply defending herself. Finally, you know important details concerning the manufacturing marijuana charge that the commenters didn't have access to because those particulars were never made public. Keep these things in mind as you read Appendix 3.

****

In Appendix 3, it's obvious that some people's imaginations ran wild. Another thing is apparent too. A few people had a lot to say. Reading the appendix made me think that several of the commenters have too much time on their hands. There is a running dialogue between several of them. It looks as though they're competing with each other. Some of them are playing the "I know more than you do" game while others are playing a game of one-upmanship—the more provocative the statement the better.

When I read Appendix 3 for the first time, I was astounded. Since so many of the commenters claimed to have first-hand knowledge about the case, I half expected to discover that Cyndi was guilty of murder despite the jury's unanimous not guilty verdict. After all, juries have been known to make mistakes. Instead, I came away from my research convinced that Cyndi is innocent and wondering why she was ever charged with a crime. I also wondered about the wisdom of giving anonymous commenters platforms from which to launch baseless diatribes.

It may be true that everyone is entitled to an opinion, but it is absolutely true that all opinions are not equal. No one should be allowed to libel others with impunity. The Internet should not be a vehicle for spewing forth unsubstantiated allegations or for skirting the laws we have in place to protect innocent people. I think the day is coming, and I hope it's not too far off, when we'll hold institutions such as *Anderson Independent-Mail* accountable for the things they publish in their online editions.

I shared my concern with Pearce Adams. He's the reporter who covered Cyndi's trial for *Anderson Independent-Mail*. He admitted that it is a legitimate issue, but that to the best of his knowledge the question has not been addressed by a court of law.

That's too bad. I can't imagine a reputable newspaper printing anonymous letters to the editor in their print editions. Why should they be permitted to publish uninformed and libelous opinions from anonymous individuals in their online editions with no risk of liability? That makes no sense to me. As far as I'm concerned, they should adhere to the same high standards in their online editions that they use in their print editions or they should suffer the consequences.

I'll go even further. I think the absence of potential consequences leads to what you see in Appendix 3, and the commenters didn't stop with Cyndi and her family. They said some terribly derogatory and uninformed things about

Druanne White too, and for one reason. She had the audacity to represent Cyndi.

Do you think they understand that in our judicial system everyone is entitled to a defense and that people are presumed innocent until proven guilty? Obviously, those nuances escaped their notice, but I'll give them credit for this much. The fact that they didn't use their real names tells me that they are sophisticated enough to attempt to hide their true identities when they post libelous accusations on the Internet. This is just a hunch, but I suspect they don't realize that the comments they post can be traced back to their computers.

Imagine how you would feel if anonymous people said about you in print the kinds of factually incorrect things they have said about Cyndi and her family…and Druanne White for that matter. Some of the comments in Appendix 3 are bizarre, literally off-the-wall, but unfortunately most of the people reading them have no way of knowing that.

Again, keep in mind that Cyndi's jury saw the evidence, all of it, and reached a not guilty verdict in less than two hours. Only a fraction of that time was spent deliberating. Cyndi knows that, but it still hurts deeply when she reads the cruel and dishonest things people have said about her and her family.

Several of the comments in Appendix 3 came from members of Amber Robey's family. My heart goes out to them. They suffered two terrible losses, but that doesn't mean Cyndi Marchbanks committed murder. I'll bet they would defend themselves if they were attacked inside their homes. I know I would, and I'll bet that you would too.

****

Earlier, I mentioned John Grisham's book, *The Innocent Man*. In it he explains that even after the verdict against Ron Williamson was overturned, the prosecutor responsible for pursuing the charges against him continued to believe that he was guilty. Scientific proof wasn't enough to convince him that the man he sent to death row was innocent. It may have been obstinacy or an ego thing. I don't know, but the DNA evidence excluding Williamson as a suspect implicated another man who should have been the prosecutor's prime suspect from the beginning.

I think stubbornness played a part in Cyndi's case too. Here's why. When I started writing this book, I tried to interview Detective Matheson, but he refused to answer any of my questions. He told me again and again that he would like to help me, but he couldn't. I tried to interview him again about a year later, and he told me that Sheriff David Crenshaw, Anderson County's sheriff at the time of the shooting, would not allow him to talk with me.

For your information, I talked with Sheriff Crenshaw before I spoke with Detective Matheson the first time. The sheriff told me that Detective Matheson could answer my questions if he wanted to. I'm not saying that Detective Matheson is being disingenuous. I'm simply pointing out what the sheriff and the detective told me.

As I was completing the manuscript for this book, I called Detective Matheson again. This time he was willing to talk with me. He spent most of his time trying to convince me that Cyndi was guilty. It had been more than two years since the shooting and more than a year since the acquittal, but he still believed Cyndi was a murderer despite overwhelming evidence to the contrary and the jury's unanimous not guilty verdict.

By that time, I had examined the law and the evidence exhaustively, so I was prepared to talk with the detective about any detail no matter how trivial. I told him that the evidence indicated that Cyndi acted in self-defense. I pointed out that the jury saw the evidence and concurred. In response, Detective Matheson said that he didn't agree with Druanne White's interpretation of the law about not having to retreat inside your home. That surprised me. I said, "Detective, that's exactly what the law says. It's not Druanne White's opinion." His response surprised me even more. He said, "I don't agree with the law."

I would never fault Detective Matheson or anyone else for holding an opinion about the law, either positive or negative. But Detective Matheson is a law enforcement officer, and his duty is to enforce the law. The detective's opinions should have played no part in his decision to charge Cyndi with murder. Did they? I don't know, but I can say this. I saw all of the evidence, and I know what the law says. The jury saw the evidence too and concluded that Cyndi Marchbanks acted in self-defense. That's an undeniable fact.

Catherine Huey's refusal to consider an option that would have allowed the drug charge against Cyndi to be expunged from her record after 3 years did not surprise me at all. The solicitor's "tough on criminals" campaign rhetoric didn't influence Ms. Huey's decision either. It couldn't have because by that time Chrissy Adams had been re-elected already.

I suppose it's possible that Ms. Huey thought she was doing Cyndi a favor by offering her a plea deal. After all, Cyndi was legally responsible for the seedlings because they were in her home. Still, the fact remains that she had nothing to do with those plants. I think justice and fairness should have led Ms. Huey to drop the drug charge against Cyndi completely since she had been tortured already…and for no reason. If Ms. Huey couldn't or wouldn't drop the drug charge, it makes sense to me that she should have allowed Cyndi's record to be cleared after 3 years.

I didn't use the word "tortured" frivolously. Cyndi lived an excruciatingly painful existence for 14 long months while she waited to learn if she would have to spend the rest of her life locked up in a state prison. At 22 years old, that must have been pure hell. And exactly what did Cyndi do? Why was she being made to endure treatment that should be reserved for bona fide criminals? She defended herself from an attacker who broke into her home and threatened to beat her to a pulp or worse. That's exactly what the evidence said, and the facts were clear on September 8, 2006. If that's not torture, I don't know what is.

Catherine Huey and the Solicitor's Office put Cyndi Marchbanks and her entire family through a grueling ordeal that no innocent person should be forced to endure. I can't imagine that Huey did it on her own initiative. I think she was following orders, but even if she was, that's not a good excuse.

****

In this book, I've done my best to be thorough, objective, and fair. That's an advantage Cyndi didn't have. I examined the evidence, all of it…carefully. That's something people in the Solicitor's Office and the Sheriff's Office didn't do. This is my conclusion. I think Anderson County owes Cyndi Marchbanks and her family a huge debt and an apology. Through their elected law enforcement officials and their subordinates, the people of Anderson County needlessly inflicted tremendous pain and suffering on the entire Marchbanks family.

That said, I think Bobby Marchbanks was right about Cyndi. She will bounce back. Even now, she's beginning to think about the college education she thought she didn't need. That's probably one of the greatest blessings in disguise she'll ever receive. In the meantime, she'll have to get used to the fact that her world has changed for good.

****

During the 14-month ordeal, Druanne White gave Cyndi copies of important documents related to her case. She carried them around with her everywhere she went in a satchel that looks like a book bag. Those documents prove Cyndi's innocence. She protected them the way a small child protects a security blanket. She showed them to anyone who was willing to sit down and take a look at them.

When I started this project, I wanted copies of several of those documents, but Cyndi was concerned about letting me borrow them long enough to make copies. I think she was afraid that I would lose them, and she didn't want to take any chances. After several months, her attitude changed completely. She didn't just give me the documents I wanted. She gave me the book bag containing all the documents and asked me to return it to her when I finished with it. I believe that shows Cyndi has already started bouncing back.

****

I want to commend Pearce Adams. The banner headline for his page one article on October 26, 2007 (the day after the trial) read "Verdict: Innocent." Actually, the verdict was "not guilty" because juries can't say "innocent," but Pearce was right just the same. Cyndi is innocent, and she knows better than most that not guilty and innocent are light-years apart.

Appendix 1

ARTICLE 6.

PROTECTION OF PERSONS AND PROPERTY

SECTION 16-11-410. Citation of article.

This article may be cited as the "Protection of Persons and Property Act".

SECTION 16-11-420. Intent and findings of General Assembly.

(A) It is the intent of the General Assembly to codify the common law Castle Doctrine which recognizes that a person's home is his castle and to extend the doctrine to include an occupied vehicle and the person's place of business.

(B) The General Assembly finds that it is proper for law-abiding citizens to protect themselves, their families, and others from intruders and attackers without fear of prosecution or civil action for acting in defense of themselves and others.

(C) The General Assembly finds that Section 20, Article I of the South Carolina Constitution guarantees the right of the people to bear arms, and this right shall not be infringed.

(D) The General Assembly finds that persons residing in or visiting this State have a right to expect to remain unmolested and safe within their homes, businesses, and vehicles.

(E) The General Assembly finds that no person or victim of crime should be required to surrender his personal safety to a criminal, nor should a person or victim be required to needlessly retreat in the face of intrusion or attack.

SECTION 16-11-430. Definitions.

As used in this article, the term:

(1) "Dwelling" means a building or conveyance of any kind, including an attached porch, whether the building or conveyance is temporary or permanent,

mobile or immobile, which has a roof over it, including a tent, and is designed to be occupied by people lodging there at night.

(2) "Great bodily injury" means bodily injury which creates a substantial risk of death or which causes serious, permanent disfigurement, or protracted loss or impairment of the function of a bodily member or organ.

(3) "Residence" means a dwelling in which a person resides either temporarily or permanently or is visiting as an invited guest.

(4) "Vehicle" means a conveyance of any kind, whether or not motorized, which is designed to transport people or property.

SECTION 16-11-440. Presumption of reasonable fear of imminent peril when using deadly force against another unlawfully entering residence, occupied vehicle or place of business.

(A) A person is presumed to have a reasonable fear of imminent peril of death or great bodily injury to himself or another person when using deadly force that is intended or likely to cause death or great bodily injury to another person if the person:

(1) against whom the deadly force is used is in the process of unlawfully and forcefully entering, or has unlawfully and forcibly entered a dwelling, residence, or occupied vehicle, or if he removes or is attempting to remove another person against his will from the dwelling, residence, or occupied vehicle; and

(2) who uses deadly force knows or has reason to believe that an unlawful and forcible entry or unlawful and forcible act is occurring or has occurred.

(B) The presumption provided in subsection (A) does not apply if the person:

(1) against whom the deadly force is used has the right to be in or is a lawful resident of the dwelling, residence, or occupied vehicle including, but not limited to, an owner, lessee, or titleholder; or

(2) sought to be removed is a child or grandchild, or is otherwise in the lawful custody or under the lawful guardianship, of the person against whom the deadly force is used; or

(3) who uses deadly force is engaged in an unlawful activity or is using the dwelling, residence, or occupied vehicle to further an unlawful activity; or

(4) against whom the deadly force is used is a law enforcement officer who enters or attempts to enter a dwelling, residence, or occupied vehicle in the performance of his official duties, and he identifies himself in accordance with applicable law or the person using force knows or reasonably should have known that the person entering or attempting to enter is a law enforcement officer.

(C) A person who is not engaged in an unlawful activity and who is attacked in another place where he has a right to be, including, but not limited to, his place of business, has no duty to retreat and has the right to stand his ground and meet force with force, including deadly force, if he reasonably believes it is necessary to prevent death or great bodily injury to himself or another person or to prevent the commission of a violent crime as defined in Section 16-1-60.

(D) A person who unlawfully and by force enters or attempts to enter a person's dwelling, residence, or occupied vehicle is presumed to be doing so with the intent to commit an unlawful act involving force or a violent crime as defined in Section 16-1-60.

(E) A person who by force enters or attempts to enter a dwelling, residence, or occupied vehicle in violation of an order of protection, restraining order, or condition of bond is presumed to be doing so with the intent to commit an unlawful act regardless of whether the person is a resident of the dwelling, residence, or occupied vehicle including, but not limited to, an owner, lessee, or titleholder.

Appendix 2

American Bar Association Model Rules of Professional Conduct (2004)

Rule 3.8 Special Responsibilities of a Prosecutor

The prosecutor in a criminal case shall:

(a) refrain from prosecuting a charge that the prosecutor knows is not supported by probable cause;

(b) make reasonable efforts to assure that the accused has been advised of the right to, and the procedure for obtaining, counsel and has been given reasonable opportunity to obtain counsel;

(c) not seek to obtain from an unrepresented accused a waiver of important pretrial rights, such as the right to a preliminary hearing;

(d) make timely disclosure to the defense of all evidence or information known to the prosecutor that tends to negate the guilt of the accused or mitigates the offense, and, in connection with sentencing, disclose to the defense and to the tribunal all unprivileged mitigating information known to the prosecutor, except when the prosecutor is relieved of this responsibility by a protective order of the tribunal;

(e) not subpoena a lawyer in a grand jury or other criminal proceeding to present evidence about a past or present client unless the prosecutor reasonably believes:

(i) the information sought is not protected from disclosure by any applicable privilege;

(ii) the evidence sought is essential to the successful completion of an ongoing investigation or prosecution; and

(iii) there is no other feasible alternative to obtain the information;

(f) except for statements that are necessary to inform the public of the nature and extent of the prosecutor's action and that serve a legitimate law enforcement purpose, refrain from making extrajudicial comments that have a substantial likelihood of heightening public condemnation of the accused and exercise reasonable care to prevent investigators, law enforcement personnel, employees or other persons assisting or associated with the prosecutor in a criminal case from making an extrajudicial statement that the prosecutor would be prohibited from making under Rule 3.6 or this Rule.

Source: http://www.law.cornell.edu/ethics/aba/current/ABA_CODE.HTM

Appendix 3
Community Comments

From "Marchbanks Not Guilty," by Amy Wood, Thursday, October 25, 2007:

- **Jenbar**: I do not agree with this verdict. I think she should have got some kind of punishment. I am really shocked, but our legal system is a mess anyway.

- **antonio**: if she was black, she would be on death row right now. if i had a gun, that accidentally drop from head and went off, and killed someone, i would be in prison for life. she shoot her on purpose.

- **Ms. Ashmore**: I feel as though Ms. Marchbanks should have been found guilty. She not only took one life but a babies life. She only got off because she is white. If it had been a black woman, they would have hung her out to dry. She may not have gotten convicted by a jury of her peers but she has to fast her maker GOD on the day of judgement. I think that no matter what kind of argument you have with someone, murder is not the way out. That is why there's law enforcement available to handle such situations. I bet Mr. Christopher Wilson will not get off for accidently killing little Javon Mayes and it is all because he is black and not that it was an accident and he was afraid. Go SC for your screwed up hidden agendas

- **Travis**: In a world with so much hate, how can the legal system let someone off with not just murder, a double murder? I lived in Anderson for several years, looks like I left just in time.

- **charmaine**: When did SC get the self defense law? This place is a mess and no one in their right minds should ever come to a state that is going to let off killers. Whose to say she will not do it again.Will she get off a second time.I think that this should be reviewed again and that Ms. Marchbanks should have to do more than cry on TV and spend a year in jail. Look at all the young men and women out there that were defending themselves and are in prison for life due to self-defense. Once again, SC does not even hold that law anywhere in the law books.I am outraged and totally disappointed in the judicial system. May God be with them all, the living and the deceased.

- **Autumn**: I dont think it had anything to do with race. Our system is screwed to the fullest extent. I know people who have went to prison for stealing. This girl killed a baby. I dont think it was self defense because she could have locked the doors and called the law. She done this on purpose. I can not believe this girl got by with murder. Had it been me, I would have let the girl beat me before I would ever pull a gun out on someone pregnant. This is crazy!

- **anonymous**: Our legal system may be not be the best....but it's part of what defines us as a democracy. This is a really tragic case, in that the lady and her unborn child were killed....but we have to remember Ms. Robey came to Ms. Marchbanks home looking for trouble and unfortunately found it. I think it is a sad state of affairs however, that homeowners are peered upon as the common criminals by prosecutors when they use force in order to protect their familys and homes.

- **Keith Cochran**: I have to respect the jury's verdict. That girl came to Marchbanks' house and she felt her life was threatened. The jury heard all the details, just remember that if we feel our lives threatened in our houses, our cars, or on the jobsite in SC, we have the right to use deadly force. That is the law. The fact that the girl was pregnant, that is so unfortunate. I feel badly about that, the unborn had no hand in it and was a victim. But I still repect the jury's verdict.

- **Ken K**: Kill and be free. This is what our legal system is telling the future murders watching and listing to this unjustice legal system. If you take a life in this case two, she should have been put to sleep faster then a dog. This was no accident. She had a gun at her disposal. she was just wating for her target. Time will past and if someone else say's some thing she does not like,she will pull out the gun and shot.

- **Mary**: I very much disagree with the verdict!! This is showing future murderers that they can get away with it. Have a "friend" come over, start a fight, and kill them, then claim self defense. She was pregnant and made to walk home, I believe I would have threatened to kick her butt too!! Im sure she was pissed!! She didnt go over there with any weapon...only herself. How can you feel that your life is in DANGER??? Maybe scared of a black eye...... The ending coulda been someone getting there butt kicked and 2 people that are now gone might still be here. People go to jail and spend YEARS for silly petty stuff and then she walks free.....sooooooo unfair.

- **Bruce**: We were not given all the testimony that the jury heard so how do you expect me to make a decision on only part of the facts of this case?

- **fuming**: Robey didn't go to Marchbanks home looking for trouble,she went to get her purse that Marchbanks took off with. When it first happened,neighbors that witnessed the shooting said they were arguing on the porch and Marchbanks went inside ,got the gun and shot Robey. In court,Marchbanks testified that her gun was approx. 8 feet inside her home where she had laid it while she waited for Robey to show up. She argued with her on the porch then went in and got the gun.She said Robey just kept coming at her is why she shot her. Coming at her from where? When it started Robey was on the porch and when it ended she was on the porch DEAD,all because of a SCRATCH on Marchbanks car window tint.

- **Anonymous2**: I am not surprised. I thought all along there was too much "reasonable doubt" to convict her. As far as the comments from someone alleging this is a racial issue, that is the most ridiculous thing you can say. She was found not guilty not because she was white, but because her lawyer did a great job creating "reasonable doubt."

- **Autumn**: Just goes to show what money can do. This is the sickest thing I have ever seen. There was NO JUSTICE, for that BABY or her mother. How can anyone say that was a fair verdict, it was a crazy verdict. She didnt even look like she was crying, she was squeling and squeezing her eyes. It makes me sick to know that someone could get off with this, and to the JURY, that was the sorriest decision ever. It will come back and get her though. There is nothing that someone can do out of spite and it not come back on them 10xs.

- **fuming**: I don't think it's a race issue,more like a money issue. Poor white people would've gotten convicted of murder too. Marchbanks' family had the money to pay a high -priced attorney.If Marchbanks had to use the public defender she would've been found guilty and gotten a life sentence.

- **justice**: i think that the jury did what they thought was the right thing… look at it as your friend comes in on you and tryes to beat you up and you know her volient past and you were so much smaller then her what would you do… protect yourself thats what

- **Fran**: I have to agree with the jury. There was to much reasonable dought. I always thought anyone had the right to protect their self in their own home. This young woman will live with the guilt for the rest of her life. This was a tragic accident for everyone involved, especially the infant. We need to let both families heal.

- **Hannah**: I totally agree with the verdict. Cynthia seemed as though she was very sorry and showed a lot of remorse during the trial. Killing her pregnant best friend was the last thing that Marchbanks wanted to do. Those of you who don't agree, definitely don't know ANYTHING about this case. I suggest you do extensive research before you begin to judge.

- **Chaz**: I agree with the jury's decision. You have the right to protect yourself in your own home if someone tries to hurt you.

- **Grace**: Personally, I totally agree and respect the jury's decision. They were there, they heard the testimonies from both sides and made their decision. Obviously, they heard facts that the rest of us did not hear and came to that unanimous decision in less than two hours. I'm glad to know that if someone comes into my home, friend or not with the intention of harming my family or myself, I have the right to defend myself and family up to and including death. I think we should let this girl get on with her life. Besides, the decision has already been made.

- **Tabitha**: Obviously those of us who were not in the courtroom do not know the facts in the case. The jury was there, they heard the facts, and they came to a unanimous decision that Cynthia was not guilty. If Cynthia had been found guilty, the laws in the state of SC would have to be changed to state that if someone breaks into your home with the intent to do you bodily harm, you have no right to protect yourself. Do we really want to give up our right to protect ourselves?

- **jenbar**: Everyone is saying she showed remorse during the trial, that was just so she could go free. Look at her personal interview on wyff4.com. During her interview she looks rather happy and no tears. Now that shes free she can really show her true side. A couple of weeks ago one of her boyfriends friend stoped by to visit them and they were discussing everything that had happened. Cynthia told him if anyone else tryed to mess with her, she would shoot them in there f*cki*g face too. So I don't think she has any remorse. This is basically teaching kids anytime you are scared someone is going to beat you up just shoot them. I am so shocked with the way things are these days. This just goes to show what money can get you. I don't agree with the verdict, but as soon as they announced Druanne White as her attorney I knew she would go free. I have to give it to Druanne she was a great solicitor and is a great attorney. I just have to wonder if she ever feels guilty for helping murderers go free.

- **disgusted**: You're right jenbar,the people that know Marchbanks know that she got away with murder. Just ask anybody that worked with her at O'Charleys.Before the shooting she was always threatening to whoop somebody's CW then after she shot that girl she described it to people like she was BRAGGING about it! No tears,no remorse ,she just seemed excited about it. The girl never touched Marchbanks,she just wanted to get her purse (that Marchbanks took off with) and she got shot in the face instead. When Marchbanks has to go to court all of a sudden she's crying and feels remorse and claims she was SCARED. The crying in court stopped when the verdict came in. If those tears were from remorse she would have been shedding some afterwards in the interview with News 4,she would shed them every time she talked about it if she TRULY felt remorse.She cried in court because she was scared she was going to prison.Now the tears are gone and she can go back to acting like a badass and will probably shoot someone else eventually since she knows how to get away with it.

- **McCauley**: Wow. I am so surprised at all of the armchair experts we have in Upstate, SC! I mean, those of you who did NOT sit in the court room and know nothing more than what the television and newspaper published (which uses propaganda to sell papers and advertising space!) have such a strong opinion and think you are right. I'm astonished! It seems to me with so many intelligent people posting here with such a knowledge about SC laws and who should and should not get off, we should have a lot more lawyers around here!

Did you ever think that it was strange that Miss Robey's face was never posted anywhere? Usually, when trying to incur sympathy for a victim, the victim's face would be everywhere you look-- think Laci Peterson, Lori Hacking, the two beautiful women in Anderson who were killed by the guy from Florida...sympathy for the victim. Why do you think Amber Robey's face was NEVER in the media? Perhaps if people had seen her they would have realized that her appearance was frightening? That she was indeed larger than Miss Marchbanks? That she would not have illicted sympathy from anyone?

I am not a lawyer, nor am I a juror, or blood-related family member of either family, but I did follow the case and I did attend the trial out of curiousity. Like many residents of Anderson County, I wanted to see what was going to happen, and like many others I pretty much had my mind made up that this young woman would do time.

Then I heard testimony. I heard for myself just what happened on that day, and I have to admit, I would not only want but expect my wife or my daughter to do the same thing under duress. Miss Robey was going in the house to attack Miss Marchbanks and Miss Marchbanks reacted the only way she could.

Miss Marchbanks is a young woman who has made some mistakes, no doubt, but she is in no way a murderer. I watched as she prayed with family and friends and this little girl, I think, will change her life after this. And as a spectator, this is not a family that looked wealthy to me, so if there is someone in the family with money, they weren't sitting in the same court room I was in!

As time moves on, I hope that you people with hate in your heart who have convicted her in your mind realize that 12 men and women, black and white, unanimously agreed this child was innocent. It is horrible that death resulted but Miss Robey was the mother of that child and only she put that infant in harm's way. Of that, I completely attest.

God Bless both families.

- **jenbar**: My family and I did attend the trial because we are friends of Marchbanks boyfriends family. For everyones information her boyfriends family is the way she got Druanne. Robey may have been larger in size but Marchbanks was not scared of her by no means. Marchbanks has gotten into it several times with Robey never did anything. The truth is she thinks she is a bad a**. If she would not have been strung out on drugs this may have never happen, although she has a violent temper anyway. The trial has only been over for 3 days, and so far she is still up to her same old ways. So for the comment she will change after this, she is still heading down the same path she was before this happen. Also just because Robey was larger in size does'nt mean she should be more afraid that does not mean anything. Marchbanks family may look like they don't have money but they could've got her an attorney. That is so funny that people always say they don't look they are wealthy, because these days the people who don't look wealthy are the ones who are. All the rich snobby looking people are the ones who go around charging everything going head over heels in debt. All I can say is Marchbanks boyfriend better watch out. Hope he never makes her mad or he may be next on her list.

- **LEISA**: This comment is directed to McCauley. You have no right to assume that Amber's appearance was frightening. She most certainly was not. For your information she had the most beautiful blue eyes that I have ever seen, her hair was gorgeous & she had a smile that would light up a room.

- **LEISA**: Although Amber was painted out to be a oversized dirty filthy scumbag monster by Druanne White, that is the farthest thing from the truth. I agree Mrs. White is one of the best that I have ever seen. But I wonder if all that money she made from helping set a murderer free helps her sleep at night.

From *Anderson Independent-Mail*, "Attorneys set stage for murder trial in Anderson," by Pearce Adams, October 23, 2007.

- **pph1234**: It seems Ms. Marchbanks was defending herself, our thoughts are with you and your family.

- **demlican**: Don't agree with the defense. Do feel sorry for her putting her famil through this. She should have been home with them instead of shacked-up with Druanne's friend's son. She was coming down off meth and wigged out on the girl.

- **ke4ada**: How much damage can a pregnant girl do? with no weapons just all mouth,Ms. Marchbanks. should have not taken the law in her own hands she should call 911 have Ms. Robey, lock up for no trasspassing, Both ladies would be doing well, may not be friends any longer MS. Machbanks, wouldnt be on trail, and Ms. Robey,would still be a live with a healthy baby girl, and probably living back with her family.

- **peaches**: IT IS WHAT IT IS THAT GIRL WAS HIGH ON SOMETHING AND EVER BODY KNOWS IT SHE NEED TO GO TO JAIL HOW CAN YOU BE SCARED OF SOMEBODY WITH KNOW WEAPON.IF THIS WOULD HAVE BEEN A DURG DEAL GONE BAD AT ANOTHER PLACE.THEY WOULD GOING TO JAIL LET PEOPLE THESE PEOPLE WERE THEY NEED TO BE.EVEN IF ITS NOT DRUGS.I FEEL SO BAB FOR THE ROBEY FAMILY.SHE NEED TO GO TO JAIL.?WHAT CAN A PREGANT WOMAN DO WITH KNOW WEAPON AND BIG GIRL STOP I THINK SHE IS TELL A LIE SHE WAS NOT SCARED SHE DONT WANT 2 GO 2 JAIL!!!!!!!!!

- **minners**: Ms Machbanks knew what she was doing!!! Because she left Ms. Robey and Mr. Jackson at the pawn shop. And had time to calm down but didn't and like all drug dealer's Ms Machbanks and her boyfriend had guns in the home with the drugs. Ms Robey being 6 month's pregant wasn't no threat to Ms. Machbanks. I feel like she should get life in prison and i don't feel sorry for Ms. Machbanks family due to they knew their daughter was on drugs and a drug dealer and is a voilent person. I do Pray that Ms. Robey family do fine Peace and Justice !!!!!!

- **pph1234**: All these comments, who knows the Marchbanks family?

- **demlican**: What does her family have to do with her and her boyfriend selling drugs and her murdering two people? Marchbanks family is from Anderson and was transferred by WAL-Mart. Her family didn't pull the trigger, Cynthia did. Her boyfriend's mother worked for Druanne White in the solicitor's office, if I recall correctly. He also has a criminal history. Question; why was there no damage to the door and it left unlocked if Marchbanks felt her life was threatened?

- **get_real**: The defense is trying to claim that Robey forced her way into Marchbanks home and was inside when she was shot but that little story doesn't add up when you could see Robey's blood puddled on the PORCH on the TV news.

- **get_real**: Not to mention the fact that neighbors witnessed the shooting and said it happened on the porch. Here's what WYFF 4 reported on Sept. 9th,2006: Friday morning, the neighbor agreed to take the couple to the pawn shop. At the shop, an argument began because the neighbor said the couple's television scratched her car, WYFF News 4 learned. The argument got so heated that the neighbor ended up leaving Robbey and her boyfriend at the pawn shop, WYFF News 4 learned. The couple walked back to their home. Robbey went to the neighbor's house to get her purse, which she left in the neighbor's car. The argument continued on the porch of the neighbor's house. According to investigators, the neighbor went inside, got a handgun and shot Robbey in the chin. Neighbors said Robbey's boyfriend performed CPR on her, but could not save her. "He was trying and he began to yell," Vera Patterson told WYFF News 4. "My grandson grabbed the phone and the man told him to call 911 and he did. He called 911 and called the law." Detectives questioned Marchbanks for about an hour before taking her to the Anderson County Detention Center. Copyright 2007 by WYFF4.com. All rights reserved. This material may not be published, broadcast, rewritten or redistributed.

- **jenn3684**: The sad thing is a couple weeks ago this girl said if anyone else messed with her she would put a bullet in there face to. Apparently she has no remorse for killing her best friend. It is so sad to see what meth is doing to people.

- **pph1234**: Gosh jenn3684, I missed that one, was it on the news?

- **pph1234**: Peaches, was that known weapons or NO weapons, I'm having a hard time reading your comment. LOL

- **demlican**: Read the article about the uninvited house guest in Pendleton. If anyone should have been shot it is that man. Yet the homeowner had more sense than to kill him. Marchbanks could have done the same thing. The officer said Robey was inside the storm door, not the door entering the house. It will still be hard in deliberations because women seem more sympathetic and men more technical. I just hope the evidence proves she was not inside the threshold of the door; that would lean more to the defense.

- **get_real**: A lot of people open a storm door to knock on the inside door. That would explain why Robey was inside the storm door.Even if she was in the threshold,she was an unarmed pregnant woman. No matter how mad someone makes you ,you can't just shoot them in an argument. It certainly sounds like Marchbanks was wigged out on meth. No rational person would become that enraged over a scratch on their car.

- **UpstateMom**: MethHead, MethHead, stupid, stupid MethHead! I hope Cynthia Marchbanks rots in a SC Dept. of Corrections facility. And to see her LOSER of an "attorney" Druanne White and her stupid assistant sitting with her during the trial, rubbing her back......makes me want to puke! The real victims here are Amber Robey and her daughter. Nobody can bring them back, but Cynthia Marchbanks CAN be made to pay for what she did.

- **demlican**: Look at Druanne White; wicked witch of the west with blonde hair.

- **minners**: Well I hope that the 12 people on the jury can sleep at night by letting a murder go!!!!! And a known drug dealer back on the street...and Ms Marchbanks stated that she wanted to get on with her life now....Well Ms Marchbanks it to bad that ms Robey and her child want even have a life because you took it and just because the jury stated that you are not guilty ...don't mean the rest of anderson resident's think you are we know that you are guilty !!!!

- **minners**: This is a good advertisement for Druanne White...If you are a killer and drug dealer just call Druanne White she will get you off and Anderson City will become unsafe.....So look out Anderson he comes the drugs and guns.

- **pph1234**: How many of you contributed to the Calvary Home for Children? Druanne was a big part in getting this done. Please try to remember all those fund raising events, or maybe you were not there.

- **demlican**: Of course I was there. Why do you think she did it? For the kids? Or maybe because some of the people that had to work for her felt

Neil Snyder

so bad for the abused child that they contributed their own money to help it. She got all the glory and the spotlight! That is all she wanted. Go ask her who else helped with all that? See if she can remember a name other than one politician who runs a drug store.

From *Anderson Independent-Mail*, "Jury finds Cynthia Marchbanks not guilty of murder," by Pearce Adams, Thursday, October 25, 2007:

- **Faieriesfun**: this is a grave in justice for a small baby. i hope marshbanks and white see that tiny face every where they look and it haunts them till eternity.

- **concernedcitizen75**: This Country is going to crap, This Murderer is walking free after killing 2 people.Either the Jurors must be Deaf and Dumb or our Solicitors Office cant present an open and shut case properly, such as this one. Anyone whom thinks this Killer should of gone Free should imagine their UNARMED PREGNANT daughter getting shot and murdered by Cynthia Marchbanks and see if you would still feel the same way. THE BOTTOM LINE IS, THE PREGNANT WOMAN WAS UNARMED AND MARCHBANKS HAD TIME TO CALL 911, SHUT AND LOCK THE DOOR OR GO OUTSIDE AND CONFRONT THE WOMAN.THE WORST THING THAT COULD OF HAPPENED WOULD OF BEEN HER GETTING HER A-- KICKED AND NO ONE WOULD OF DIED AND THE UNBORN BABY WOULD OF GOTTEN BROUGHT INTO THIS WORLD and this would of never occured. WAKE UP MORON JURORS and THOSE OF YOU GLAD SHE WALKED! HOPE THE JURORS SLEEP WELL KNOWING THAT THEY ALLOWED JUSTICE TO GO UNDONE.

- **concernedcitizen75**: DRUANNE WHITE DON'T PLAN ON RUNNING FOR THE SOLICITORS OFFICE ANYTIME IN YOUR NEAR LIFETIME. YOU LOST ALOT OF VOTERS WHO WOULD HAVE VOTED FOR YOU BEFORE.BUT DON'T WORRY OUR CURRENT SOLICITOR WON'T BE GETTING THE SAME VOTES SHE RECEIVED LAST ELECTION AS WELL. MS. ADAMS IS NO BETTER.

- **ClemsonGirl**: Where is justice in the state of South Carolina?I mean this is CRAZY!!!!I cannot believe this murderer is walking our streets!I have been following this case since day one.First of all, Cynthia could have called 911 if she felt threatened.I mean Amber was a six month pregnant woman,

160

how much harm can she inflict on a person?And to Cynthia, if you felt that threatened why not shoot her in the foot, you shot her in the face, with a good aim I might add with your eyes closed.It's just hard for me to believe that Amber was Cynthia's best friend since childhood and yet Cynthia could still take her best friends life despite that.Not only did she take her best friends life but that innocent baby also.What kind of message are we sending to the citizens of Anderson County?Scratch my window tint and It is ok to kill someone?What about the manufacturing of marijuanna in Cynthia's home?I suppose that is Amber's fault also huh?It's funny you used to see good old Druanne White defending murder victims now she is defending these murderers.What a great reputation she has made for herself now!Its lawfirms like Ms.White's that are getting these crazy people like Cynthia Marchbanks off and making Anderson County an even more dangerous place to live!Cynthia Marchbanks you may have got off of a murder charge but you have to spend the rest of your life living with the fact you killed two people, that is indisputable.The Bible says "Thou Shall Not Kill".This whloe country is in a mess,ther is no justice anymore.Good job Druanne White Law Firm you have done nothing more than send out a message to all of the rest of these gun happy people in Anderson County that it is ok to kill a human being over something so petty!

- **alexanderregan29**: Well she may have received her freedom now. When its time for judgement what do you think will happen. Until then she knows the truth and hopefully it will consume her life and she will be miserable. There is no justice left in this life, but there is after life.

- **Judy_in_SC**: The fact that Amber was Cyndy's best friend speaks to her defense. She must have felt that her life was in danger in order to resort to using a gun. I know Cyndy and have seen firsthand the pain and anguish this has caused her. And why attack Druanne? Both lawyers presented the facts in a courtroom which was presided over by a judge; and the verdict was determined by a jury. If the prosecutor couldn't convince the jury that this was murder, maybe it's because the facts did not support that theory. No one is disputing the fact that Cyndy pulled the trigger, only whether or not she acted in self defense. In this country we are presumed innocent until proven guilty; the facts of the case could not prove Cyndy guilty. Her life will forever be affected by her actions on that day. I pray that all the people affected by this tragedy will be able to one day find peace.

- **flytyerace**: This is not a grave injustice. Both ladies had the choice to stop and both stay at home. She took the life of her on child in her own hands.These are life choices. LIFE choices. People need to pay attention on how you will react when you are faced with this type of confrontation.

- **minners**: People say that they know Ms Marchbanks ...Then you know that she is a drug dealer and her boyfriend is and that she is a volient person and don't care about anyone but her self...and Ms Marchbank knew what she was doing and I hope the guilt eats at her for the rest of her life...and Ms Marchbanks stated that she wanted to get along with her life now...It's to bad that Ms Robey and her baby want be able to get on with her life... and I hope that Ms Marchbank moves to another state due to the 12 jurys don't speak for the rest of the Anderson Resident's and we don't want another drug dealer and killer back on the streets... and for as Druanne White she want get any votes if she ever runs for the solicitors office and what people don't know is that Ms Marchbanks boyfriend mother works for Druanne White so that tell's it all!!!!! Ms Marchbank you are a killer !!!!!!

- **minners**: Ms Marchbank was crying on stand and kept crying in the courtroom ...but the real reason that she was crying is because she was scared to go to jail ...not because she felt bad for killing Ms Robey....I pray for the Robey Family to fine peace after all of this....Because they are the ones that lost alot!!!!! and is the ones that are in real pain!!!!

- **yessirbird**: Don't vent your frustration at Druanne White. She did a heck of a job defending Ms. Marchbanks. If you want to blame people, blame the voters of Anderson County for voting the best dang solicitor out of office. Now Druanne White is the best dang defense attorney in Anderson County. I don't think anyone has to worry about Druanne running for office again. She could not afford the pay cut.

- **powerstroke**: I will agree that this is a very tragic case where two people lost their life, especially the unborn child, but if I had been on the jury I would have voted the same way (Guess I'm just another MORON in Anderson). The moment Amber came through the front door into the

162

house after Cynthia is what made this case end with a "not guilty" verdict in my opinion (Yea I know what people say about Opinions too). I know if I'm in my home and someone comes in it after me I will use whatever means I have to defend myself. From the start Druanne White said it was a case of self-defense and she stated she would prove it and she did. Also as far as the charges of manufacturing marijuana I think she and her boyfriend should face those charges too, but I don't think Druanne White would win a "not guilty" verdict on it.

- **minners**: True!!!Druanne White does get payed very while to put the murderers and drug dealers back on the streets of anderson ....and one day it will come back to her and her supporters due to evil doesn't hold any barrier from rich to poor ...evil get's anyone it can!!!!!

- **yessirbird**: minners, You sound like a moron. The accused have the right to a defense. It is the system. Would you suggest that we not have defense attorneys?

- **Kat39**: You folks out there haven't watched enough Law & Order. What you don't know about this case is that the pregnant woman was high on drugs at the time of the attack. She was a drug abuser. But, you don't hear about any of that because the judge through it out as prejudicial, I imagine, and because the media is too biased to print it. If you want to blame someone, blame the pathetic Solicitor's office and Chrissy Adams, for their lack of understanding of the law and their in ability to prosecute cases. Druanne White is the best solicitor Anderson County ever had with the highest conviction and closure rate in the entire state during her tenure. Now, she is the best defense attorney in Anderson and probably the state. And whoever said she would never run for office is correct.....why would she? In private practice, she doesn't have to worry about the ignorance of the public and the bias of the media. Congrats Druanne and Ms. Marchbanks.

- **flytyerace**: Ms. White did what she was supposed to do. What on earth would you do if your DEFENCE attorney did not DEFEND you. This is getting turned around. Ms. Robey went into Ms. Marchbanks home. As far as the child, Ms. Robey should have thought about that before. But that was not as important to her as it is to the rest of us. Everyone is mad. Put the anger where it belongs.

- **get_real**: Marchbanks testified that the gun was 8 FEET inside her home,that she got it and Robey kept coming at her and when Robey was 12 INCHES away she closed her eyes and shot her. That means Robey would've had to walk 7 FEET inside the home to be 12 INCHES away from where Marchbanks claimed the gun was. Yet Robey was shot on the porch and the neighbors witnessed it. The neighbors gave a statement at the time of the shooting saying both women were on the porch arguing and Marchbanks went inside and got the gun. The argument began on the porch and it ended on the porch with Robey DEAD in a big pool of blood. If the jurors AREN'T morons then they must've been asleep to think this was a case of self defense.

- **Kat39**: get_real, I sure hope no one ever steps on your property and threatens you. If I had to defend myself, no matter how far away the perpetrator is, I will shoot first and then worry about where I am standing later. In addition, I hope that I can get someone like Druanne White to defend me and jurors that can see the truth for what it is. Until you have listened to every piece of evidence and been in that jury room talking about the fate of someone's life, don't pass judgement. You have no idea what you would.

- **get_real**: Kat39, I HAVE been in a dangerous situation where I was threatened by a man, not an unarmed pregnant lady!I had the the common sense to call the police instead of my BOYFRIEND. Marchbanks knew Robey would be coming over,that's why she laid the gun on the entertainment center.She could've been calling the police during that time but her excuse was she didn't want to get Robey in TROUBLE! She chose to KILL her instead!

- **SCPrincess**: I would just like to say (and everyone is free to reply rudely or whatever), I knew Cyndi. I worked closely with her. There was very few days on the job that she didn't get volotile or hostile against one of her co-workers. She constantly threatened to take them to the parking lot. Most of us were not surprised when this incident occurred. We all saw it coming for a long time just didn't know who it would be against. I talked to her when she made bail. I didn't see remorse for her actions. I saw excitement when she told me the story. She was getting angry all over again. Now, as for the mother being on drugs, that was her mistake. Going into Cyndi's house was also a mistake. But, the facts remain. Cyndi was a loose cannon that didn't need much pushing to go off. In this case, she should've called the police or someone she knew instead of premeditatively putting a gun within reach so it would be ready. Not to mention the plants found growing in her house. If it had been anyone else, simple possession of a small amount would end up in at least some jail time. She got nothing. She was in the wrong and should've been punished. Two lives were taken that day. One belonged to an innocent baby. I hope her attorney is happy with that accomplishment. And to those who are coming down on the rest of us for seeing facts, I'm sorry you're too blind to see the truth. The woman was unarmed. She was alone. To try and decide what happened that day is impossible cause no one was there to see it. So, all we have are the facts.

- **yessirbird**: SCPrincess said "I hope her attorney is happy with that accomplishment." Thanks. I will respond rudely. What an asinine statement to make! I don't think any rational person would be happy about the loss of that baby, especially Druanne White. Do you know how many sick perverted rapists and child molestors she put away when she was a prosecuting attorney? She can't stand to see a child hurt. So, quit attacking the attorney. She did her job. Again, every accused person is entitled to have a defense.

- **concernedcitizen75**: Kat39 and yessirbird you are a bunch of IDIOTS and must have a Druanne White fan club, thats why you keep kissing her A--. The only reason why she won the case is because she knows how to work the system in her clients favor and more power to her and yes our current solicitor isn't worth a damn and hopefully will get replaced next election. If either of you had any Brains or a Soul you could see Bottom line. This Pothead Killed 2 living people because she was scared to get her butt kicked, not because she was in fear for her life. Ms Robey had NO weapons and was 6 months Pregnant. If Marchbanks would of done any of the following this would of never happened, #1 call 911 #2 Lock the door and don't answer it, #3 answer the door go outside and get her a-- whipped #4 In worst scenario SHOOT her in the LEG or FOOT, she's alot better shot than me to hit her in the face with her eyes closed. Any of these and the cemetary would have 2 less plots filled. IDIOTS like you 2 are why people like this get off the hook and laugh about it later. If that was your daughter that happened to , your stupid views would be different.

- **demlican**: If you're going to shoot someone, wait till they are within arms length. That is the law! Otherwise, it is not. Druanne said she was a foot away, why do you think Cynthia OPENED the door to let her in. If she was so scared, she would not have opened the door. I was not in the courtroom and did not hear what evidence the judge would not let the jury hear. They had to reach a verdict based on the facts presented; beyond a reasonable doubt. Druanne is a witch, putting it nicely. She learned how to defend from prosecuting. All, pretty much all, attorneys go to work prosecuting before defending. Good defense attorneys are good actors and liars. They really don't want to know the truth because it would be considered unethical. Chrissy could be a defense attorney. She resigned while working for Druanne and told her she would run against her. She did and beat her. Chrissy has always been a prosecutor and can also remember her victims. Druanne will not even remember Marchbanks in a month. She has no feelings for others; just herself. She and her office is corrupt. Her kids are on drugs, her ex assistant who is now a judge still sits with her in court; do you really think she is not getting a break? Don't worry about her having nightmares because she has no empathy or sympathy for no one. She worries about herself. She does nothing that does not get her attention. I will vote for Chrissy Adams anyday before I will Druanne or one of her ex employees. If you need to talk to Ms. Adams, call the office, she never shuns anyone. How often do you see her trying to get on TV or in the newspaper. She takes care of business like a solicitor should. Maybe she could hire better attorneys to prosecute the cases, but she don't have to be in the spootlight. The facts were presented in court and the fact that it took Amber 20 minutes to walk home, Marchbanks had plenty of time to leave if she didn't want to call 911 and get Robey in trouble. If she was so scared, why not call 911 instead of your boyfriend, who in turn called his mother who worked for Druanne. Marchbanks was not scared of Amber when she ordered her out of her car. Robey apparently got out, Marchbanks didn't have to throw her out. None of it makes sense! Marchbanks is getting her free meds now because of all her anxiety. Don't have to worry about getting busted with them. I hope the family of the baby sues Marchbanks civily. It would work. Just because you're not guilty in criminal court doesn't mean you're not in civil court. Fact; she took the life of two people, meaning to or not. Look at OJ Simpson. I would even help them with attorney fees. Lastly, I would rather have a prosecutor as a friend than a defense attorney; they believe in right and wrong and just like Marchbanks, their reputation and justice for the victims, depend on those 12 people that are on the jury. It truly is a sad day when they let a killer go free.

- **demlican**: Go to WYFF4 and watch the whole interview. She is already on her Xanex and Druanne is there with her. She said she did everything she could do to prevent it. DUH, she didn't call the police or leave. That is not everything possible. She wants to be an attorney like Druanne she said, while looking up at her during the interview. Sickening!!!

- **kitkat4u**: I am so afraid for my kids now knowing that we have a defense attorney like Druanne and people like those on the jury in this case. Thanks for not only letting a drug dealer go free but a murderer as well. I can't understand why anyone would let someone go free that said, "i didn't want to get her in trouble," but turn around and kill her instead. Please people, what could be worst, getting someone in trouble or killing them? I think Marchbanks was scared of getting her ass kicked more than fearing for her life. I see a lot of people talking about the facts, well the facts was there and Marchbanks should have been found guilty---guilty!!!! I feel so bad for the victims family and I will be praying for them for a peace of mind. I say leave it to God and let Him handle everything/everyone. People like Druanne, Marchbanks, and the jury will have to live with the decisions they made and I promise you, God is not pleased with them at all!!! May God blessed those who really got hurt from all of this---the victim and her family!!!

- **kitkat4u**: I say this world is in so much trouble and we all really need to pray. Anderson is getting terrible and I hope that this case doesn't influence people to think that they can get by with "murder" if someone does something as small as damage their "tinted windows." I really think this case will make it even worse to live in Anderson especially with all the drugs, robberies, and murders going on. Thanks Druanne and the jury for making Anderson an even more dangerous place to live!!!!! There goes one drug dealer and murderer set free, how many more will there be?

- **get_real**: Anderson will just keep getting worse as long as they let the violent criminals go free. The cops arrest them and then the court turns them loose. All you have to do is read the arrest reports and you see some of the same names over and over and over for assault,burglary,selling drugs,etc. Some repeat offenders rack up 10 or 15 felony charges ,then when they go to court they plead guilty to ONE and the court dismisses all the others. That's what happened to 3 young men in Homeland Park that kept getting out on bond and continued to sell drugs and steal from people.One of them wound up on FOX News charged with Trafficking Meth after he'd already been charged with distribution of meth and a list of other charges. All 3 of them got a slap on the wrist and only have to serve 2 or 3 years. They're scheduled for release in 2008 so it won't be long their names will be in the arrest reports again!

- **yessirbird**: concernedcitizen75, Look no further than your mirror to see the true idiot. The point again, for you slow people, is everyone is entitled to a defense. If it was not Druanne, it would have been someone else. BTW, is her defense attorney not supposed to defend her? The process played out and you are not pleased with the outcome. The jury made the decision. Instead of taking cheap shots at the defense attorney that did her job, maybe you need to be an advocate for changing judicial proceedings. Try to make a change where defendants are not represented by an attorney or either they are only represented by the law school drop-outs.

- **kitkat4u**: yessirbird...You sound like one of those who have needed a defense attorney before. Of course Druanne is doing her job, but how to you go from putting the bad in jail to defending them? Maybe she saw that she could make more money by defending the criminals than putting them in jail. And i do give the police props for doing their job but it beats all odds when the criminals are set free by the system---that really sucks!!! If I were a cop, I would feel that I waste my time catching the criminals if the system sets them free. It's not fair to them(cops) or the community, but i guess "money" speaks louder than words!!!!

- **kitkat4u**: I listened to the tape on WYFF4 that Marchbanks made but there is still no excuse. Like concernedcitizen75 said, there were other steps that could have been taken to prevent Marchbanks from killing her friend and her unborn baby. If someone fears for their life: 1st--call the police

2nd--don't answer the door(a 6 month pregnant woman couldn't kick the door in) 3rd---if you have a gun, wait to see if that person does enter the house forcefully(before using the gun). My thing is, there were neighbors that seen the argument on the porch between the two ladies so the door was already open and Marchbanks went back inside to get the gun on her pregnant unarmed friend. Sounds like to me the jury was asleep!!! I just thank God that I don't have "friends" like Marchbanks. And to SCPrincess you should have went to the prosecutors with the story that you told here to be used on the behalf of Marchbanks character. She sounds violent to me and have shown how violent she could be.But then again, SCPrincess, I can see why you didn't. Maybe Marchbanks would have been after you next!!!!

- **wethepeep**: It all boils down to job performance. The prosecutor did not present the people's case as well as the defense attorney. Apparantly the defense framed the best story of how it all went down. I'm concerned about the solicitor's office. This should have been cut and dry. The jury was made up of common every day folk that live and work in Anderson and probably have the same ideals as most of us do. They heard the evidence presented and came to a consensus based on the evidence they heard which I'm sure they took very seriously.

- **kitkat4u**: wethepeep...You are so right. The prosecutors must have done very poorly at presenting their case. This does no justice for the people,Amber and her baby. It's sad that it all went down like this but life is full of surprises and this is definitely a surprise. I think most of Anderson was looking for a guilty verdict---I know I was!!!! I can't even imagine how Amber's family feel!

- **demlican**: As I said earlier, I wasn't in the courtroom and do not know what evidence was presented; therefore, I can't say if Druanne was better or the prosecution. The judge is the one who says what the jury can hear. But I do say, the jury is suppose to be your peers. If you are a drug dealer do they pick, pick I mean select drug dealers, if your are a murder of a certain age do they select people of your age? No. If there is a civil case about a faulty product where there is expert testimony about how the product works, do you think they go select all engineers who know the working of the product. Course not. These are random people who have no clue of what is really going on. Define peers and it someone close to the same age, same social and cognitive skills, and same intellectual skills. The defense has the upper-hand because they have more strikes than the prosecution. Meaning if it someone they don't think will think the same as they do, they strike them. That is the system. The defense gets 15 and prosecution 10. Marchbanks is lucky her parents paid an attorney rather than a public defender. PD is a second job to their own business. That is why you have idiots on a jury.

- **demlican**: SC Princess, they should have had her coworkers on the jury; "peers" if you will. Do you think the verdict would be the same? NOTA in hell. I know her and her boyfriends family. You're not telling me anything I didn't already know. People need to remember the jury is suppose to be of your peers; high school peers are people around you at that age with the same intelligence and skills. It is not the prosecutions fault. They are actually the minority in trials.

- concernedcitizen75: yessirbird(brain), you and your fellow Moron kat39 are the couple of few Idiots supporting the murderer Marchbanks, get your head out of Druanne White's rear and get some air. You obviously don't have children and can't fathom what it would be like to have someone shoot them dead and their unborn child all because Ms. Marchbanks didn't want to get her A-- kicked. You probably would do the same thing she did because your probably some coward that would sh-- in your pants if someone bigger than you came to your door wanting to whoop your A--.I notice you yessirbirdbrain and Kat39 have screenames named after animals,are you two related or is it because you have the same mental capacity as those animals.

- **ClemsonGirl**: AMEN...."helpkidsfirst"!I totally agree with you.To Amber Robey's family PLEASE file a civil suit against that sick murderer Cynthia Marchbanks.You will win it.It is indisputable that she killed Amber and her unborn child.Look at OJ Simpson, he was found not guilty(which we all knew he was)and Ron Goldman's family won their civil suit in court.Justice may not have been served but I would hurt Cynthia Marchbanks in her pocket by suing her sorry butt!Oh yeah,and to NEWS 4 all you guys are doing is giving this sick low life of a person all of this publicity instead of the Robey family.They are the ones who lost not

Marchbanks.It was so funny to watch Cynthia in the court room and cry freakin rivers the whole time but in the interview with NEWS 4 after being found not guilty she dried up real quick like!She cried like a baby the whole time in the court room because she was scared her sorry low life self might be going to jail for life not because of the loss of Amber and that innocent baby.I noticed Cynthia said in her interview that she is ready to get on with her life and perhaps go to school and be a low life lawyer like Druanne White.Well good luck to you Cynthia because every where you go in this town everbody knows your face and nobody will give your sorry butt a chance at any descent job or anything else for that matter!

- **SCPrincess**: Yessirbird, In reply to your comment and the others you have posted, the only idiot here appears to be you. Do you know Marchbanks personally? I did. All I hear you say over and over to everyone is that a person deserves a defense and her lawyer did her job. None of that is relevent to the subject. A killer went free. She got her defense. Yes, the lawyer did her job. She got paid for doing it. It's just hard to believe that someone who fought against crime at one point in her life could go so far as to defend a case that obviously shouldn't even be argued over. It's cut and dry. She was guilty. Now, instead of saying the same thing over and over like you have been, try addressing the issues that the others here have commented about. Make sense out of why she didn't call the police. Why she answered the door. Why she placed a gun near the entrance as if waiting for what turned out to be a "big accident" in her mind. Accidents happen. This was something she completed steps to facilitate. Grow a brain and start seeing the big picture here. I'm not just someone commenting on what I saw on the news. I knew both girls very well. I was their manager. So, you can crusade all you want but face facts. And if you choose to post anything else, try posting something that addresses everyone else's questions. Why she didn't call the police. Why she opened the door. Why she put a gun near the door in anticipation of Amber's arrival. The problem with people like you is the same as the liberals. They show up in the middle of something, give a suggestion and walk away. They don't have the first clue what's going on or how stupid they sound. Get the facts. Get a clue. Then post something sensible. To everyone else, good work! At least the majority of the people on this comment board believe in justice. That means that all of society hasn't gone down the drain!

- **SCPrincess**: To Kitkat4u, Yes, that was a concern for me for sure! But, I feel bad every day that I didn't go and testify. I wasn't asked or anything but should've requested it. I was on vacation when it happened and when a co-worker called and told me, I broke into tears. It was so hard to believe that something like that could just happen. I stand with you and the others. There were many options that could have been used besides killing her! It wasn't fear that caused this. It was anger. She let rage push her to take two lives.

- **SCPrincess**: To Helpkidsfirst, I agree completely! A jury shouldn't be made up of a group of people who know nothing other than what they are "allowed" to hear by the court. It should be by those who knew her best. I think if they had gone about it that way, there's no way she would've been innocent. I know people might think that I hated her but that's far from true. I tried to help Cyndi and tried to be her friend. I wanted her to get control of her emotions. But, I also feared that something bad would happen because of her constant rage. She knew what she was doing. She was guilty.

- **get_real**: SCPrincess, Another question that needs to be answered is "What happened to the neighbors that witnessed the shooting ?" They couldn't possibly have testified because what they saw completely contradicts Marchbanks story. And for the people that actually BELIEVE it happened the way Marchbanks said : When faced with the fact that she could go to prison,what would you expect her to say? Would you expect her to ADMIT that she killed Robey in a rage? That Robey just came to get her purse and she shot her in the face because she was still in a rage over her scratched window tint? Of course not! She'd have to be a complete idiot to admit that. So she claims self defense and hires an attorney that knows just what to do to trick 12 jurors into believing that it may POSSIBLY have happened as Marchbanks claims.

- **SCPrincess**: Yeah, I wondered why the neighbors weren't brought in. Maybe they didn't want to risk getting involved. She definitely got lucky. Half the evidence wasn't presented and the people who knew here weren't called. Good thing for her it can't be brought up again cause she couldn't get that lucky twice!

- **FamilyTies**: Kat39, Medical reports signed by the coroner show that my cousin had no drugs in her system at all. Quit spreading your lies. Cynthia got off, because of the lies told by her witnesses. They said my cousin tore the screen door off of the hinges and stormed inside. Yet, the Forensic Investigators stated that there was no damage to the house at all. They also stated that Amber was shot on the porch, not in the house. After two hours, the jury returns a 'not guilty' verdict. I bet the jurors were all friends paid by the Marchbanks family.

- **SCPrincess**: I would just like to know if Kat39 and yessirbird are friends of hers, know her, or are they just story followers! Lol

- **pph1234**: Amber smoked pot the night before she was killed.

- **SCPrincess**: Wow.. A crime punishable by death for sure! That's a warning to everyone out there. If you happen to catch a buzz, fear for your life!! Wonder what Marchbanks was on all the time to make her the way she was on a daily basis?

From *Anderson Independent-Mail*, "Anderson County might not face its second murder trial in less than a month," by Pearce Adams, October 31, 2007

- **kc73**: i cant believe they found this marchbanks girl not guilty it was 2 girls on drugs fighting i just got done with jury duty glad i was not on this jury. how do those people sleep at night not only was a woman murderd but her baby to. what is this country coming to i guess amber really knew how to fool all of u . u let her get away with murder. u should really be proud of your self.

- **FamilyTies**: kc73, I think you made a mistake. Amber (my cousin) was the one killed. Cynthia Marchbanks is the one they let off scott free. It is a shame the criminal justice system is not like it was in Bible days. Marchbanks would have been found guilty for sure. And her sentence would not have been freedom, I can guarantee that. Druanne White and Marchbanks will have to live with it until they stand before God. He won't be as lenient as that jury was. Marchbank's interview was a joke. She was not the same tearful crybaby she was the day before. Matter of fact she seemed to be enjoying herself. The tears in the courtroom were put-on.

- **get_real**: 2 girls fighting????It was 2 girls arguing,all mouth ,no blows were exchanged .It became a physical altercation when Marchbanks grabbed her gun and shot Robey. If they had actually been fighting,then Marchbanks defense may have been a little more believable.

From http://www.topix.net:

- September 14, 2007: I am Amber's mother, I have read all the response's some nice some bad. Amber will be gone nearly 1 year shortly. I have to say I miss her more than anyone could ever imagine. I spend my day's searching for the right answer's. There are none at this point,I will never see her or my grand daughter ever again. I held Hailey in my arms the day she passed away.Another hurtful sorrowful moment, she was a little angel she couldn't tell me grandma I hurt,she couldn't cry,she was beautiful, the last part of Amber. I have Hunter and of course he asks where his mommy is, this is very hard to explain. She's with God is all I can tell him right now, he is so young, to young to know what happened to his mommy.It has taken 1 year to come out and talk, so its very painful. I wanted to respond to some of the remarks, but I decided not too. The good Lord will make the final say,and I have faith in him.

- September 18, 2007: me and my wife and kids knew the Marchbanks family pretty good back when they lived here in Anderson from the early-mid 1990`s. they went to our church. cyndi s daddy bobby marchbanks worked for years as a grease monkey in sears. her momma gwen worked at wal-mart. gwen got bobby a job as auto center manager at wal mart. he had a reputation for being charming, quick tempered and a cut throat. i saw him treating his employees bad many times at wal mart. Cyndi`s mother gwen was very wierd and strange. you have to wonder how all of this affected cyndi. she was a sweet shy girl at our church. i know that her daddy bobby really enjoyed guns and constantly talked about how many annimals that he had killed. the marchbanks moved away and we haven t seen them around anderson for many years. were they rough like this up in maryland? i wonder how much their actions messed up cyndi. have cyndi s parents bobby and gwen moved back to anderson? when did cyndi get into drugs?

- September 18, 2007: Bobby was a hunter & Ive never met a hunter who did not brag. Gwen did not allow her children to have nor play with guns.

As far as tempers we all have them. Although I guess if you can read, we have decided to make this topix a mutual site. Say positive things or move along. If you would like I can meet you in church. I would like to print your comment and see if your preacher teaches about judging people. You say Marchbanks at our church. So I assume your a member. I know the bible says thought shalt judge. I will pray for you.

- September 28, 2007: I have read this board since the beginning and I've had to listen to a lot, but I never posted anything. I've always been able to just say to myself that TWO people know the truth, TWO families were torn apart, and emotions are such that we're all guilty of letting them override our common sense. BUT, I cannot believe anyone would call Bobby Marchbanks a violent person! Bobby is like my brother. We grew up together in the same house, with him only 9 years older than I. For years, he was my hero. I adored him. He doted on me and loved me so much. Bobby is an avid hunter. However, he has never been violent towards any other human ever. He is a remarkable, charasmatic, intelligent, and charming man, but never has he been known as dangerous or defiant. His children are nothing more than blessed to be raised by such a loving, caring, and responsible man. You are misled in your belief, "marchbanks at our church" and you should be ashamed for posting such LIES.

- October 4, 2007: Mentally unstable? Possibly. Mentally damaged? Maybe. Emotionally scared? Could be. Mentally retarded? Absolutely not. Cyndi is a very smart girl who made a very studpid decision. What happened is tragic. The decision she made was the wrong one. We shouldn't even be talking about it because it never should have happened, it's all just plain wrong. And without comparing sob stories I will say this, my family has faced tragic life altering events as a result of someone elses actions and it was so painfully hard to move on through the grief. What I have found to be helpful was remembering that karma is real. She will suffer, she will face judgement, she will be punished. Sending out negativiity towardss her only brings it back to you, have faith that every action has a reaction and the appropriate one will come back to her.

- October 7, 2007: I went to high school with Bobby Marchbanks and did buisness with him over the years at the different Auto Centers that he worked at. I think that the poster that was in their church was just exploring answers on why Cindi Marchbanks pulled the trigger and killed a mother and her unborn baby. I can see where the church members that last saw the Matchbanks in the mid 1990`s, would be shocked that shy little Cindi killed two people. This is an open public form where (thank god) people are free to express their feelings and beliefs. You might not like what they say, but it is their right to say it. Bobby Marchbanks was a good man when I knew him. He, like everyone else has a private side that is different from what you may see everyday in public. That is just saying that I believe that he was a good father and very providing and caring for his family. However, in high school Bobby really only watched out for what was best for Bobby. He would be someone`s best friend in the world , if he could gain something from you or you could benefit him in some way. Let`s just say that he was one to really talk about others behind their backs. The church poster who knew the Marchbanks family was just wondering how all of this affected Cindi growing up. Bobby adopted Cindi in the mid 1990`s. He and Gwen have two other younger daughters together, Cindi was the oldest child. Gwen (cindi`s mom) was not very outgoing and somewhat a recluse. One can only wonder how all of this affected Cyndi. I believe that they are good parents and do the best that they can. However, I do remember Bobby talking about the guns that he carried around in his vehicle. He was one to let his temper get the best of him sometimes, even in high school.

- October 7, 2007: How in the hell has Cyndi Marchbanks stayed out on bail for over one year? How did she even get bail at all? How would a judge in his right mind give her bail? What is her mental state? What has she been doing for the past year? iS mARCHBANKS still a wattress?

- October 9, 2007: There has been no new info. about this case or about Marchbanks in almost a year. I too am frecked out that she has been running around loose on bail. I hope that I don`t run into her at whatever restaurant that she is a waitress at. She sounds like a crazy psycho. Why would she do something like this? What has she contributed to the Anderson community since this. I also wonder if she has still been dealing drugs out of her crack house home. She was living in sin with Justin Bond. I wonder what her church goings parents thought about that. Roosevelt Street is an old mill area. I wonder if she moved there with her shack-up boyfriend because it was a good place to sell drugs.

- October 23, 2007: Drom reading the previous messages , its sounds more like Cynthias family in on trial. How ridiculous. It is sad the way that things happened in this situation but its a reality that you face when drugs are a part of your life. Both parties(Marchbanks and Robey) were on drugs. This argument was about something so stupid as scratching window tiny. Both parties are just as guilty as the other for allowing it to escalate to the point that it did. Cynthia knew the scratch on her car was not that big of a deal as well as Amber knew that going to Cynthias house would only cause more trouble. Amber endangered her own life and her babies by making that choice to go to her house.(as I recall neighbors saw her force entry into the home) People say she was going to get her purse which had already been left a Ambers house. All sides need to admit that this was a sad unfortunate incident where lives were lost due to each parties ignorance. Cynthia in no way sounds like a cold blooded murderer and now she may spend her entire life behind bars because of something so stupid just as Amber is now dead as a result of her poor decisions.All this is about to most peole is seeing Cynthia suffer by going to jail but what does thatsolve? Nothing. She is not a murdering beast as some had made her out to be. This wasa situation of someone defending theirself at their own home which is legal. Amber should have returned to her own home and left the argument alone. But as many do she could not quit. Cynthia was very stupid fo rpulling out a gun but if she was afraid then can you see how things like this happen? Many people have guns in their homes and never harm a soul but if someone is banging my front door down and I am afraid then I will protect myself. That is just what Cynthia did. Leave out all of the details of drug use and dealing because that falls on both parties involved. When it comes right down to it, they both lived a sorry lifestyle and now they have paid dearly for that.Cynthia should recieve a light sentence for what has happened and Amber should have never went over there to begin with, sad that she paid with her life for her stupidity.

- October 23, 2007: Well now, I can understand where you want to defend Cynthia,but how dare you come on here to say that Amber paid for her life for her stupidity! Why come on here and pretend that you are trying to understand how both of them went to a certain level of anger. I just won't believe that Amber would have walked into a "bees nest",because she was "stupid"!Amber went over there to get her purse,which she didn't know was suddenly on her porch.The two of them were friends so why in the world did a gun have to play in the situation to begin with. I think you better wait and let the courts decide what Cynthia's fate be,and stop "hating" on a dead girl who is not here to defend herself!

- October 24, 2007: Both of these girls, Deceased Amber and Crazy Cynthia were hooked on a life of hard drugs, sex without marriage and drug abuse. Maybe this was all too much for these two families to deal with. SOMETHING made them move to Anderson, Sc to an old mill village where they were involved in heavy drug selling and abuse. And yes, both girls seemed abessed by cheap sex as both were unmarried living with questionable male companionship. Amber`s boyfriend was on TV and had a large tatoo on his neck. The girld were letting their sex drives and drug hunger influence their lives.

- October 24, 2007: ok what u are saying makes no freakin sense what to ever amber was getting planing on getting married to her boyfriend so before you get on here and post dumb comment know wtf u are talking about and because her boy friend had tatoos on his neck that makes him some evil person .... heres what you need to do take your head out of your ass go back to church re-read your bible and pray to god to forgive your for being a dumbass. why u are there also rememeber about passing judement without facts.... people like you is why this country is so fucked up in the 1st plac.

- October 25, 2007: The jury has fond Cynthia Marchbanks NOT guilty! Go to www.wspa.com or www.wyff.com for the stories. Hopefully, Cynthia and her garbage family will leave South Carolina and go back home to Maryland. There is no place for that slime her. Alot of people hate anything to do with the Marchbanks family because of the not guilty verdict. I think that they know this and Anderson has seen the last of all of them forever. They are taking the trash back to Maryland.

- October 25, 2007: I just found out the news about Cynthia being found not guilty,as for South Carolina laws state you have to prove without a reasonable doubt! I hurt for my sister. She had to suffer deeply when Amber was killed,and now she has to suffer once more. I wasn't there and neither were alot of people,but the way that Ambers name was strung through the mud makes this whole mess a travisty.I hope God gives my sister and her husband strenth to carry on,and hope that now they can start the healing process. I think that justice was not served,but I can't make or change the system. I also want to state if Cynthia was found guilty,I didn't want her to get a death penalty. I don't believe in death penalties or murder, I do believe in incarceration for a heinious crime.

- October 25, 2007: As I have read through the messages on this board, I simply cannot believe that some people would lower themselves to this level. Neither family needs this right now. While Cynthia may not have been found guilty, she will have to live with what happened for the rest of her life. And the Robey family will miss Amber everyday. Nothing could make this situation right. No ammount of time served will bring Amber back. On the awful day that this took place, two people let things go too far. Amber should have stayed at home and Cynthia should have locked herself into a room to call 911. But hindsight is always 20/20. If either girl were able to go back and do it again, Im sure they would. Sadly though the world does not work that way.

  What has happened is so unfortunate for everyone involved but to call either family trash because of the way they lived their lives is ridiculous.Everyone makes mistakes and no one has the right to judge another. I know both families and they are both full of wonderful people. The Marchbanks family nor the Robey family is trash. They are both families who have been deeply affected by this terrible tragedy.They deserve to be left alone. Neither of these girls nor their families deserve to have their names drug through the mud like this. The jury has made a decision based on evidence presented to them. That does not mean that Cynthia and her family should have to move from Anderson. She was found not guilty therefore she should be able to go on with her life as normal. Had different decisions been made on both girls parts that day , they would both be continuing on with their lives right now. Just let it be over and allow both families to heal. They do not need to hear a repeat of this everyday, they will relive it in their minds everyday because I am sure it was hell on both families. Just let it go and allow them all to move on the best they can. I honestly thought Cynthia would have served some time but apparently the jury felt there was not enough evidence in this case. Maybe it was only in self defense , Cynthia is no more of a murderer than Amber would have been if things would have been the other way around.

- October 26, 2007: Cynthia needs to stay down there where people say screw whats right and protect the locals. because in the real world she is a cold blooded killer. it would be so funny is she was to leave SC and have a chain with a rock attached to her feet and she was droped into the middle of the atlantic ocean. i mean if its ok to defend yourself with a gun when

179

the person is unarmed then that should be legal also the great thing is that she will always be looking over her shoulder wondering if someones out to get her. the only reason she was found innicent is because the laws in SC are from the stone age no way should this have ever been self defense and the not guilty is just locals taking care of there own i hope they all get whats coming to them in the end. btw none of this is threats it would just be what comes to bad people imo.

- October 26, 2007: Wow..........

  I am speechless...I am in tears and I am disgusted.

  I am ashamed that I live in a Country where lives are held at such little value.

  I am also sick to my stomach that Chester woke up everyday to defend a countries freedom only so people like this can walk free.

  Amber you will be missed by anyone whom ever had any contact with you.

  I will continue to pray that the Robey family will find peace in knowing that while our justice system has failed to hold her accountable she still has one more person to answer to that is bigger than all of us and knows what happened that terrible day.

  It saddens me that Cindy will get to go on with her life....possibly change her life for the better, have the opportunity to have children and a family but at the same time- it is truly in that moment that she herself becomes a mother that she will understand the pain that she has caused Kathy.

  RIP Amber and Hailey

- October 26, 2007: My thoughts and prayers are with Ambers friends and family. I cannot fathom the pain you will forever feel, I hope you can find the strength to carry on down a positive path in life, keeping Amber and Haileys memory alive in light.

  We weren't there when it happened, we weren't educated with the evidence and facts, we cannot judge. No matter how you feel about the decision that was made please try and remember that two families were struck by tradgedy and no amount of nastiness or anger will change anything that happened.

May everyone have a blessesd day.

- October 26, 2007: I am a memeber of New Prospect Church in Anderson, SC where the Marchbanks family attended until they moved from Anderson in 1995. A poster on here said that Cynthias parents are rich, they are not. They make a good living, but are by no means rich. Most people here are shocked that Cynthia got off. I am heard it from good sources that the Marchbanks family is trying to get daddy Bobby transferred somewhere in NC. There they can be away from Maryland and South Carolina but still in the South. I just never trusted these people even though we attended the same church. I have heard some other things in the church about them that would make your head spin. If you are around the Marchbanks, I would distance myself asap. They are really very dangerous people, even though they try to always coming out smelling like a rose. We don`t want them in Upstate Sc.

- October 26, 2007: I have known the Marchbanks family for quite some time and they are far from trash and who are you to say what we want in SC? Many people agree that it was self defense. Of course Ambers family would not agree because they lost her. This is a terrible situation but to say the Marchbanks are dangerous is completley ridiculous. They are no more dangerous than any other family in SC. They love Cynthia just as Ambers family loved her. Both girls had their faults but neither deserved what has happened. Sadly enough this does sound like self defense and most of it could have been prevented if Amber had only walked away when confronted with a gun.   Obviously Cynthia was afraid otherwise why would she have shot her?   She is far from the cold blooded killer that people on here are making her out to be.   She showed alot of remorse for what has happened while the very people on here who are complaing are only worried about talking badly about each girls families.   You should all let this go and move on the best way that you can.   It is over now   and   the   verdict   is   done..

The other comment about tying a block to Cynthias legs was uncalled for. You should know that makes you no better than what you are claiming Cynthia to be.Very sad. Whats even worse are the people wh oare claiming to know the Marchbanks from church as JUDGING them. Your church should teach you better than that. If you ever really knew either family, you would know that they are good families who have just been through a horrible ordeal.

www.ingramcontent.com/pod-product-compliance
Lightning Source LLC
Chambersburg PA
CBHW060302290526
45789CB00001B/381